Materials for Teaching Adults: Selection, Development, and Use

John P. Wilson, *Editor*

Materials for Teaching Adults: Selection, Development, and Use

John P. Wilson, *Editor*

NEW DIRECTIONS FOR CONTINUING EDUCATION
ALAN B. KNOX, GORDON DARKENWALD, *Editors-in-Chief*

Number 17, March 1983

Paperback sourcebooks in
The Jossey-Bass Higher Education Series

Jossey-Bass Inc., Publishers
San Francisco • Washington • London

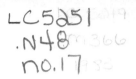
John P. Wilson, (Ed.).
Materials for Teaching Adults: Selection, Development, and Use
New Directions for Continuing Education, no. 17.
San Francisco: Jossey-Bass, 1983.

New Directions for Continuing Education Series
Alan B. Knox, Gordon Darkenwald, *Editors-in-Chief*

New Directions for Continuing Education (publication number
USPS 493-930) quarterly by Jossey-Bass Inc., Publishers.
Second-class postage rates paid at San Francisco, California,
and at additional mailing offices.

Correspondence:
Subscriptions, single-issue orders, change of address notices,
undelivered copies, and other correspondence should be sent to
New Directions Subscriptions, Jossey-Bass Inc., Publishers,
433 California Street, San Francisco, California 94104.

Editorial correspondence should be sent to the Editor-in-Chief,
Alan B. Knox, Teacher Education Building, Room 264,
University of Wisconsin, 225 North Mills Street, Madison,
Wisconsin 53706.

Library of Congress Catalogue Card Number LC 82-84181
International Standard Serial Number ISSN 0271-0579
International Standard Book Number ISBN 87589-943-9

Cover art by Willi Baum
Manufactured in the United States of America

Ordering Information

The paperback sourcebooks listed below are published quarterly and can be ordered either by subscription or as single copies.

Subscriptions cost $35.00 per year for institutions, agencies, and libraries. Individuals can subscribe at the special rate of $21.00 per year *if payment is by personal check.* (Note that the full rate of $35.00 applies if payment is by institutional check, even if the subscription is designated for an individual.) Standing orders are accepted.

Single copies are available at $7.95 when payment accompanies order, and *all single-copy orders under $25.00 must include payment.* (California, Washington, D.C., New Jersey, and New York residents please include appropriate sales tax.) For billed orders, cost per copy is $7.95 plus postage and handling. (Prices subject to change without notice.)

To ensure correct and prompt delivery, all orders must give either the *name of an individual* or an *official purchase order number.* Please submit your order as follows:

Subscriptions: specify series and subscription year.
Single Copies: specify sourcebook code and issue number (such as, CE8).

Mail orders for United States and Possessions, Latin America, Canada, Japan, Australia, and New Zealand to:
Jossey-Bass Inc., Publishers
433 California Street
San Francisco, California 94104

Mail orders for all other parts of the world to:
Jossey-Bass Limited
28 Banner Street
London EC1Y 8QE

New Directions for Continuing Education Series
Alan B. Knox, Gordon Darkenwald, *Editors-in-Chief*

CE1 *Enhancing Proficiencies of Continuing Educators,* Alan B. Knox
CE2 *Programming for Adults Facing Mid-Life Change,* Alan B. Knox
CE3 *Assessing the Impact of Continuing Education,* Alan B. Knox
CE4 *Attracting Able Instructors of Adults,* M. Alan Brown, Harlan G. Copeland
CE5 *Providing Continuing Education by Media and Technology,* Martin N. Chamberlain
CE6 *Teaching Adults Effectively,* Alan B. Knox
CE7 *Assessing Educational Needs of Adults,* Floyd C. Pennington
CE8 *Reaching Hard-to-Reach Adults,* Gordon G. Darkenwald, Gordon A. Larson
CE9 *Strengthening Internal Support for Continuing Education,* James C. Votruba
CE10 *Advising and Counseling Adult Learners,* Frank R. DiSilvestro
CE11 *Continuing Education for Community Leadership,* Harold W. Stubblefield
CE12 *Attracting External Funds for Continuing Education,* John Buskey

512437

CE13 *Leadership Strategies for Meeting New Challenges,* Alan B. Knox
CE14 *Programs for Older Adults,* Morris A. Okun
CE15 *Linking Philosophy and Practice,* Sharan B. Merriam
CE16 *Creative Financing and Budgeting,* Travis Shipp

Contents

Editor's Notes   1
John P. Wilson

Chapter 1. Educational Materials for Teaching Adults   5
Wesley C. Meierhenry
Decisions about using a learning resource should be made within the context of
the instructional plan.

Chapter 2. Audiotape and Videotape Materials for Professional   13
Development in Mental Health
Peter Geib, George R. McMeen
Audio and video materials can enhance employee career programs and im-
provement of services to the public.

Chapter 3. Slide Sets: Development and Selection   21
for Use in Teaching Adults
David J. Miller
In selecting slides and developing slide sets, keeping some basic principles in
mind will improve the quality of this visual treasure.

Chapter 4. Designing Instructional Media for Attitudinal Outcomes   29
Michael R. Simonson
Media can change attitudes. Six guidelines for effectively using films for atti-
tude changes are provided.

Chapter 5. Material for Learning and Acting: Video and Social Change   37
Thomas W. Heaney
Interactive use of media, especially television, is a source of learning material
in liberatory education.

Chapter 6. Computers and Materials for Teaching Adults   47
Problem Solving
Rex A. Thomas
It is difficult to sufficiently coordinate formal instructional experiences with the
work environment to permit adequate integration. Computer models can pro-
vide needed experience in an instructionally optimum manner.

Chapter 7. Materials for Nontraditional Study and the Natural   53
Learning of Adults
Charles A. Wedemeyer
Mass produced material must be made effective across a wide span of individual
differences in order to stimulate and sustain idiosyncratic learning.

Chapter 8. Educational Materials Development and Use with   **61**
Self-Directed Learners
Susan T. Rydell

Self-directed learning is controlled by the learner, not the educational materials
or the provider agency.

Chapter 9. Self-Assessment in Educational Programs for Adults   **69**
Leo Goldman

Informal self-assessment methods must focus on the positive (seeking strength
and growth) rather than seeking negative factors in the person's life history.

Chapter 10. Adapting Materials Use to Physical and Psychological   **77**
Changes in Older Learners
Don C. Charles

Age related, psychological developments among older learners effect their
reception, processing, and responding to information.

Chapter 11. Selection and Use of Materials in Adult Basic Education   **85**
Literacy Instruction
Florence W. Carmen

Selecting materials for teaching is challenging, because today there are more
than 150 publishers of ABE materials.

Chapter 12. Evaluating Educational Materials   **95**
Richard L. Holloway

A method for evaluating instructional materials is presented which considers
learner attributes and instructional characteristics.

Chapter 13. Where Do We Grow from Here: Synthesis and Discussion   **103**
John P. Wilson

A summary and discussion of the sourcebook and implications for practice and
research.

Index   **111**

Editor's Notes

The amount of material for use in teaching adults literally has exploded during the past few years. Most conventions for educators provide rows of exhibits and displays of books, pamphlets, films, slide sets, worksheets, tests, and computer programs. Further, most hardware stores, lumberyards, craft shops, and grocery stores have available many pamphlets on topics that range from hanging a patio door to dieting to buying or building solar collectors. All of these materials are available from sources in addition to the traditional ones, such as libraries, schools, museums, and film repositories.

Along with this increased availability of materials comes a series of important questions. Foremost among them are questions such as: How do I know what to use with whom? How do I use it most effectively? How can I be sure the materials are educationally sound? Is there a highest and best use of certain kinds of materials compared to other kinds? What should I pay attention to as I develop materials for use in teaching adults?

This sourcebook has several purposes. The first purpose is to address questions like those above in order to provide assistance in selecting appropriate materials from the vast array available: printed, audio, visual, or combinations. The second purpose is to provide assistance in developing or adapting educational materials to various settings. To these ends, several authors discuss their experiences, successes, and failures in using educational materials in specific situations. For example, Geib and McMeen explain the use of audiovisual materials for staff development at the Southeast Mental Health Center in Fargo, North Dakota. Carmen discusses some of her conclusions about selecting and using materials in adult basic education (ABE). Her chapter reflects her experience using materials with ABE learners. Simonson reports some of his research on the use of films. He concludes that the nature of what is on a film in terms of credibility, relevance, and arousal potential is as critical as the procedures followed in using the film for attitude change.

The foregoing chapters are helpful in both selecting and, to some extent, developing materials. Several chapters emphasize developing materials. Meierhenry presents an overview of the use of media in instruction. He then considers some features of adulthood that have implications for what media might be effective with adults. Miller provides a step-by-step procedure for developing and embellishing slide sets for effective use in teaching adults. Charles discusses the need to adapt materials to psychological changes in older learners that involve receiving, processing, and responding to information.

Wedemeyer raises some intriguing questions about mass-produced materials and their potential for effectiveness among a highly individualized learning society. If we develop materials on the basis of "where the learners are," do we risk learner regression rather than progression? Rydell extends some of Wedemeyer's implications to self-directing learning materials while pointing out the paradox between self- and other-directedness. Goldman provides further suggestions for helping learners individualize their self-assessment. His discussion about the use of informal methods for self-assessment of values, beliefs, and self-perceptions are particularly relevant to adult and continuing education programming for personal development.

A third purpose of this sourcebook is to push beyond the common parameters and perceptions of what constitutes educational material. Whereas each author alludes to this issue, the context of their discussions for the most part are in what has been seen as traditional instructional settings. Meierhenry sets the stage for alternative views of educational contexts; Wedemeyer, Rydell, and Geib and McMeen go a little farther. However, Thomas, in discussing materials for use with computers, indicates the need for instruction to be more concerned with individuals' histories of experiences in order to be most effective in teaching a problem-solving process. Heaney pushes even farther, stating that videotaped educational materials are most effective when they are produced by the learners who are to use the material for their collective learning.

This sourcebook is organized around four general sections. The first section is devoted to media materials, with Chapter One starting as a general overview. Chapters Two through Six are each devoted to a specific medium. The second section focuses primarily on printed and individualized materials, with Wedemeyer reflecting upon individualizing mass educational materials in Chapter Seven. Chapters Eight through Eleven discuss specific individualized materials in specific provider-agency settings.

Chapter Twelve presents a procedure for evaluating educational materials. Although the focus here is on printed matter, there seems to be great potential for the application of the procedure to various materials. For example, Holloway suggests incorporating various aspects of the instructional process in an evaluation of materials. Each preceding chapter identifies some of the aspects to include in this evaluation process.

This sourcebook reviews concepts and procedures for the selection, development, and adaptation of many types of materials for use when helping adults learn. It also provides examples of their use in a variety of provider agencies, since the term *continuing education* includes adult education, extension, training, and human resource activities.

This volume concludes with a consideration of future directions for continuing educational materials. The benefit of this volume depends on the extent to which continuing education practitioners adapt some of the ideas to their own situations.

John P. Wilson
Editor

John P. Wilson is professor of adult and extension education and extension specialist-education at Iowa State University. He graduated from the University of Wisconsin–Madison, where he studied instructional theory, group dynamics, and learning in adult education. He has developed and published many educational materials and workbooks. He has also used these materials extensively for teaching in various continuing education programs.

*The use of various materials is necessary if all instructional goals
and objectives are to be realized by all learners. Decisions about
the nature and types of resources to be used should reflect
consideration of a number of factors.*

Educational Materials for
Teaching Adults

Wesley C. Meierhenry

This sourcebook is an attempt to assist continuing educators in making decisions about the selection and development of teaching resources. There are many types of resources currently in use in continuing education. In this publication, for example, specific chapters deal with films, slide sets, and interactive television, while other chapters deal with many other types of materials. Additional examples illustrate both the variety of resources used in continuing education and the various types of continuing education agencies that are using various technologies.

A recent article in *Fortune* magazine titled "Trends in Computing: Applications for the '80s" addresses applications of computers to business and industry, but the implications for education (including continuing education) are clear and distinct. Some idea of the speed and extent of this development is found in the following:

- Over the next five years, United States businesses will spend over a trillion dollars on information processing.
- The industry is growing at an average yearly rate of 16 percent, with many sizeable sectors running at 25 percent and higher.
- By 1986 there will be over eight million computers installed in the United States, over seventeen million terminals, and over five mil-

J. P. Wilson (Ed.). *Materials for Teaching Adults: Selection, Development, and Use.* New Directions
for Continuing Education, no. 17. San Francisco: Jossey-Bass, March 1983.

lion word processing/electronic typing workstations—over three times the number of keyboards in place today.

The effectiveness and uses of this technology in continuing education have been considered but are untested (Chamberlain, 1980). Thomas (Chapter Six) presents a view for teaching problem-solving processes as an effective use of computers in education. Heaney (Chapter Five) describes a process of interactive video for a liberating education similar to Freire's use of slides for this purpose. In many cases, the combination of television and computers, and the use of telephone systems with and without computers, are becoming part of the educational system (Chamberlain, 1980).

Although there is considerable use of various new materials and resources in continuing education today, there is some resistance to their extensive and widespread use by some practitioners. The instructional model used by many continuing educators is based upon the small-group approach. Many continuing educators who follow such a model view the use of these new materials as being divisive and not contributing to the desired dialogue and discussion between the mentor and learner.

Others fail to use certain materials because of time and economics. Commercially prepared materials are not always available and some continuing educators either do not have the skill to produce them or do not have access to material production centers. Others fail to use such materials because they just do not believe they are necessary for successful teaching.

Rationale for Use of a Variety of Materials

The decision to use a particular learning resource should be made within the total context of the instructional plan. The decision to use a certain type of material should be made because, to attain an objective, the experience presented by the resource is crucial to an understanding of the material to be learned. In this writer's opinion, the use of pictures and slides by Paolo Freire as a part of the conscientization process, which he defines as "development of the awakening critical awareness" (Freire, 1970, p. 19), is the best example of how a medium is essential to an outcome.

Freire and his colleagues found that slides or pictures that are carefully selected and properly presented are the only means available to help individuals see their environmental surroundings in a new and detached manner. Therefore, slides and pictures are essential to the process of conscientization—the development of critical awareness of one's environment.

For Freire, it was pictures or slides; for the instructional objectives of other continuing educators, it may be motion pictures, simulations, or audio materials. In any case, the resource should not be an "add-on" feature but should be an integral part of the learning experience.

Some Variables to be Considered in Choosing Materials

A variety of factors should be considered by the teacher when instructional decisions are being made concerning the selection and use of learning resources, in addition to the characteristics of the material itself.

Age. The age of the learner should be kept in mind during the selection and use of resources. Chapter Ten of this volume considers materials for teaching older adults. It is well known that many older adults have a certain amount of hearing loss, for example. Further, Schaie, in a recent presentation (1982), argues that older adults have difficulty with processing visual information as rapidly as younger adults. He indicates, for example, that, unless interstate highway information signs are placed considerably in advance of the physical entrance and exit ramps, older adults will have difficulty in processing the information with sufficient speed to make appropriate decisions. Thus, it is critical that continuing educators be aware of the characteristics that affect both the type of material chosen and its utilization. A longer screening time for transparencies, for example, should be considered when using this medium to teach older adults if the information is to be adequately processed.

Educational Background. There are great differences in the types of materials used with learners at various levels of formal education. Undereducated adults (see Chapter Eleven of this volume) prefer many more concrete and first-hand experiences in order to learn. Because such individuals do not work well with abstractions, the materials should be much more first-hand and experience-based, such as field trips, community study, and, in some instances, activities such as games and simulations. Professionals participating in continuing professional education will respond well to abstract and complex materials because they have the background to understand and interpret such materials. Such individuals can work more easily with symbolic materials like readings, intricate drawings, graphics, and flow charts, which assume an extensive background for understanding and interpretation.

Ethnic minorities have backgrounds conditioned by the cultures from which they come. Therefore, educational materials should take into account both the affective and cognitive domains. Such individuals have strong feelings about the manner in which minorities are depicted in the material and value judgments about minorities inherent in the materials. Thus, instructional materials should avoid stereotypes and portray minorities and both sexes operating at the highest social and economic levels. In addition to the affective elements of the materials, certain ethnic groups learn best with experience-based materials, others with visual materials, and others with dramatizations. For example, a major educational device with the Vietnamese is social drama.

Foreign-born adults have some learning problems similar to ethnic minorities, but, in addition, their native languages frequently have linguistic bases much different from English. The educational materials used with such learners should be both concrete and experience-based, as described above, but should also give consideration to how to translate ideas and meanings from the native tongue to English. Materials and methods used with such learners differ according to the ethnic group and the similarities or differences in linguistic base between the native tongue and English.

Learning Styles. Learning styles describe students in terms of those educational conditions under which they are most likely to learn, which suggests that certain educational approaches will be more effective than others. There are several different opinions about what elements pertain to learning styles; consequently, a variety of scales or tests are used to classify students.

One approach is that of Kolb (1976), who concluded that we perceive information along a continuum from concrete to abstract. Those who tend to be at the concrete end of the continuum sense and feel their way to knowledge, while those who tend toward the abstract use thought to perceive information. Kolb also concluded that some learners process perceptions by reflecting and watching, while others jump right in and try them out.

When these two dimensions are juxtaposed, four learning styles emerge. Type One learners perceive concretely with their senses and feelings and process reflectively by watching. They are known as reflective sensor-feelers. Type Two learners perceive with the intellect and process reflectively by watching; they are called reflective thinkers. Type Three learners perceive with the intellect but process by doing and are known as thinking doers. Type Four learners perceive concretely with their senses and process actively by doing; they are called doers.

If all four learning styles are represented among adult learners, then it is evident that learning materials should vary from concrete experiences (Type One) to intellectual and abstract experiences (Type Two). Research completed with fifth- to twelfth-grade students (McCarthy, 1981) has found that the majority of preparatory education is addressed to the Type Two learning style, while only 28 to 30 percent of the students have such a learning style. There is reason to believe that more adult learners fall into Types Three and Four; they prefer to be active learners and they perceive with the intellect, concretely. Hence, most continuing education teaching approaches should plan for active learners.

Cognitive Styles. There are also a number of approaches to cognitive styles, including that of Witkin (1977), who classifies individuals as learner-independent and learner-dependent. According to Witkin, learner-dependents require much more structure in educational materials than do learner-independents, who intuitively develop structures and categories. If one is teaching a group of learner-dependents, the materials should have more structure built in to them (for example, transparencies used with overlays help learner-dependents induce a structure into their learning experiences, while learner-independents naturally induce structure into materials, even if it is not included in them).

Regardless of the learning approach or cognitive style, an analysis of the categories into which learners are divided reveals major differences in how materials should be developed and utilized. If various styles are found in an adult class, as is generally the case, then the teacher or facilitator should use a variety of materials, both concrete and abstract, and offer opportunities for both reflecting and doing.

Sex. The sex of the learner is likely to make a difference in the type of material chosen. Research on cognitive styles, discussed earlier, has concluded that, in Western culture, women show small but persistent differences in the direction of field dependence, in contrast to males, who are more likely to be field-independent. Because field-dependents tend to view things holistically and are gregarious, affectionate, considerate, and more people-oriented, it is obvious that such learners feel more comfortable in small discussion groups and in face-to-face kinds of learning activities, where sharing of experience dominates. Field-independents, on the other hand, are more likely to deal successfully with abstractions, parts as well as wholes, and are not highly people-oriented. It should be pointed out that both males and females may be either field-independent or field-dependent, and so the instructional decision about a particular material cannot be made only on the basis of sex.

Hemispheric Specialization

Since at least 1961, when Sperry peformed surgery on a forty-eight-year-old war veteran who had suffered severe brain damage, there has been much speculation that the right and left hemispheres, or lobes, of the brain perform quite different functions. The findings popularized the split-brain phenomenon, and led to Sperry's reporting, "Both the left and right hemisphere of the brain have been found to have their specialized forms of intellect. The left is highly verbal and mathematical, performing with analytic, symbolic, computer-like logic. The right, by contrast, is spatial and mute, performing a synthetic spatio-perceptual and mechanical kind of information processing that cannot yet be simulated by computers" (1973, p. 31).

In recent years, a number of questions have been raised about the findings and the generalizations that have followed them. First, it appears that the two lobes of many learners seem to perform more or less equally, so that there is not always a clear distinction as to which lobe dominates. Second, some researchers have argued that almost all learning acts require some input from each lobe. For example, in order to read, it is necessary to process the visual symbols, even though the content is verbal. More recently, some researchers have argued that there is evidence that the different functions of the two lobes, as described by Sperry, are a matter of culture. Such a hypothesis suggests that the differences in how the lobes of the brain process information hold true for white middle-class Americans, but research on individuals of another culture (such as the Japanese) suggest that they process information quite differently from the way reported by Sperry.

Even if the two lobes of the brain do not process verbal and visual information completely differently, there is sufficient evidence that, in the American culture, at least, different functions are performed by the left and the right lobes. Materials thus should be chosen to appeal to each lobe, including both verbal and visual materials utilized in a linear and holistic manner, because people do vary in their preferred modes of learning.

Content

In addition to the learner characteristics discussed in the preceding section, the choice of materials should also take into account the nature of the content being taught. For example, if the content is from such areas as science or mathematics, the choice of material is more likely to include the opportunity to present structure (such as the use of transparencies). On the other hand, if the field is the fine arts or the humanities, then the type of material to be selected is more likely to be open, less structured, and more holistic; it might include commercial television programs, music, or drama presentations. The emphasis in the fine arts and the humanities is to have learners form their own impressions and judgments rather than having uniform concepts imposed from the outside.

Thus it is clear that the choice of materials and resources is related to the subject matter being taught and also dependent upon whether the objectives are mainly in the cognitive, affective, or psychomotor domain.

Conclusion

The selection and/or development of appropriate instructional materials is crucial to successful adult learning. The task is made more difficult today by the vast array of materials available.

From the many different types of materials available, continuing educators should select those that are best fitted to such learner characteristics as age, educational background, ethnic background, country of birth, learning styles, cognitive styles, sex, and type of hemispheric specialization. In selecting materials, the nature of the content being taught has implications for the type of materials selected and utilized. Finally, the choice of materials is affected by whether the learners will be individuals, in a temporary group, or in an organizational or community setting.

Recognizing these influences, successful continuing educators use various tools to assess learner characteristics and preferred learning styles. They also analyze the nature of the content and how it needs to be presented to be learned, consider the arrangements of the learners, and consequently select or develop appropriate materials.

Therefore, the choice of materials becomes integral to effective instruction, and their use is essential to accomplish learning objectives. Materials used under these conditions are not add-on activities, but an integral part of the instructional plan. Materials used as a result of such planning promote increased dialogue and interaction among learners as well as with the leader. They provide the impetus and motivation that make useful and pertinent human interactions and lead to meaningful learning.

References

Chamberlain, M. (Ed.). *Providing Continuing Education by Media and Technology.* New Directions for Continuing Education, no. 5. San Francisco: Jossey-Bass, 1980.

Freire, P. *Pedagogy of the Oppressed.* New York: Seabury, 1970.

Kolb, D. E. *Learning Styles Inventory: Technical Manual.* Boston, Mass.: McBer, 1976.

McCarthy, B. F. *The 4 Mat System: Teaching to Learning Styles with Right/Left Mode Techniques.* Arlington Heights, Ill.: Mark Anderson and Associates, 1981.

Schaie, K. W. "Cognitive, Bio-Social, and Psychological Development of Adults: A Research Perspective." Address to Adult Education Research Conference, Lincoln, Nebraska, April 1, 1982.

Sperry, R. W. "Left Brain, Right Brain." *Saturday Review,* September 9, 1973, pp. 30–32.

"Trends in Computing: Application for the '80s." *Fortune,* May 31, 1982, pp. 22–24.

Witkin, H. A. "The Role of the Field-Dependent and Field-Independent Cognitive Styles in Academic Evolution: A Longitudinal Study." *Educational Psychology,* 1977, *69,* 197–211.

Wesley C. Meierhenry is professor and chairman of the Department of Adult and Continuing Education, Teachers College, University of Nebraska–Lincoln. He is a past vice-president for Field Services of the Adult Education Association of the U.S.A. He also is a past president of the Department of Audiovisual Instruction of the NEA (now Association for Educational Communications and Technology— AECT). He received the Distinguished Service Awards presented by Adult and Continuing Education Association of Nebraska in 1981 and AECT in 1980. Meierhenry has written and consulted extensively on the use of materials in adult education.

Audio and visual material can enhance components of career development and education focused upon employee training and improvement of public services.

Audiotape and Videotape Materials for Professional Development in Mental Health

Peter Geib
George R. McMeen

Research in continuing education suggests that audiotapes and videotapes are useful avenues of instructional communication. These media may be used to advantage in the development of a staff improvement program that can lead to employee growth and better services.

Both audiotapes and videotapes were used in instructional delivery systems for a staff development program at the Southeast Mental Health Center in Fargo, North Dakota. The program served the professional needs of psychiatrists, nurses, psychologists, gerontologists, chemical abuse counselors, and social workers. The use of audio and video materials is of particular interest because it can enhance career development, education, and training of employees and thus improve services rendered to the public.

The Staff Development Program Model

Essentially, the staff development program is directed by the chief executive officer of the health organization, who receives input from depart-

J. P. Wilson (Ed.). *Materials for Teaching Adults: Selection, Development, and Use.* New Directions for Continuing Education, no. 17. San Francisco: Jossey-Bass, March 1983.

ment directors and the staff development coordinator. Staff development committee members are appointed by department directors, who select these members from staff ranks. The committee advises the coordinator on matters concerning the planning and implementation of three professional development tracks that form the program: (1) individually negotiated career development goals, (2) in-service training, and (3) continuing education.

Annually, department directors and the committee assess the needs of agency employees who are served by the department's programs. The coordinator is responsible for studying agency staffing needs and available resources in light of organizational goals and for making recommendations to the chief executive officer, who is ultimately responsible for the planning and direction of staff development programs. This model for staff development allows the organization's department directors, staff development committee, staff development coordinator, and chief executive officer to work together to attain the organization's professional development goals and those of individuals working within it. A consensus-building approach similar to the one suggested recently by Lippitt (1982), in which the coordinator of continuing education and staff development is directly responsible to the chief executive officer, was a key factor in the successful implementation of such a staff development program and its three professional development tracks at the Southeast Mental Health Center. Burke (1982) indicates that the organization's intent should be to foster a flexible attitude toward the individual's professional growth and to maximize staff proficiency in serving clients and the community in a way that also serves to educate staff members about the organization's purposes and role.

Rationale for Using Audio and Visual Materials

In considering the various alternatives for instructional communication, staff developers and instructional program planners have considered audiotapes and videotapes appropriate for facilitating instruction and learning. Thorman (1976) noted that, as measured by posttests, off-campus, continuing education students who used audiotape to complement weekly discussions were as knowledgeable as on-campus students who attended traditional lectures and discussions. In addition, the off-campus students felt as positive about their learning experience as did the on-campus students. The research findings of Popham (1961), Menne, Klingensmith, and Nord (1969), Stanley and Reich (1974), and Wasson and Thorman (1975) led to similar conclusions about other groups of students. On the basis of pretest and posttest scores and student evaluations of course and instructor, Thorman (1975) found no significant difference between the performances of continuing education participants taught using a videotape-discussion method and those of on-campus students taught by the lecture-discussion method. These findings are supported by other research (Pollack and others, 1956; Klapper, 1958; Berger, 1962; Bickel, 1965; Thorman and Amb, 1972; Thorman, 1974). Thus, on the basis of the general conclusions of these studies and particularly those of Thorman (1974, 1976) that relate to off-campus continuing education, audiotapes and videotapes were viewed as viable vehicles for disseminating information in in-service training and continuing education.

Examples of Instructional Materials

At the center, audiotape and videotape materials were used as instructional resources and instructional delivery systems. Audiotape cassettes served both purposes, while videotapes were primarily used as a means of instructional delivery. The convenience and ease that attended the use of audiotape cassettes contributed greatly to their dual purpose. When they were available as instructional resources, they generally were expected to have information of a singular nature for the various professionals at the center. Consequently, audiotapes might contain special information from workshops, seminars, and conventions or be recordings of guest speakers at these or other organization-hosted events and activities. When audiotapes were used as an instructional delivery system, they provided lecture-type information appropriate to each of the three staff development tracks. Videotapes were used in a similar way to present information that supported the instruction and training program. Case studies and special presentations that required the use of visual materials were often recorded and made available as instructional components for in-service training.

A successful approach to the use of audiotapes in higher education has been the Audio-Assisted Independent Study method, which demonstrates that students learn as effectively by listening to lectures recorded on audiotape cassettes as they do by attending regular class lectures. Wasson and Thorman (1975) reveal that students learn just as much from cassette instruction and feel as positive about their courses and the instruction when they learn in this manner as they do with conventional instruction that relies on the traditional lecture method. For example, students attend three half-day meetings in addition to listening to audiotape cassettes in place of lectures. The first of these half-day sessions introduces the course to the students and provides an opportunity for pretesting; the second session has a class discussion and an opportunity for the instructor to check student progress; the third session is reserved for posttesting or the administration of a final exam. Courses based on this method have been a part of the continuing education program at Moorhead State University, Moorhead, Minnesota, for several years; however, they have not been related to any mental health staff development program. The success and popularity of this method demonstrates that continuing education courses can indeed be taught in this manner. Thus, in-service training and continuing education programs in the mental health field could benefit from the use of audiotapes and videotapes in conjunction with some method for instructional organization, such as Audio-Assisted Independent Study. The advantages of this or similar methods would include the following:

1. Professional staff could proceed at their own learning rates in using either medium in individualized instruction.
2. Staff members could learn at a convenient time and place of their own choosing.
3. The content of audiotape or videotape recordings could be played back for review.
4. Economies in transportation could be achieved in some regions where instructor and students would normally be expected to travel to a designated site for regular class meetings.

Certainly, an important consideration in the use of an adaptation of the audio-assisted method would be that instruction and attainment of professional goals might be more accessible and achievable for a larger number of staff members.

Development Procedures for Instructional Materials

If a consensus approach to professional staff development is followed, peer review will be an important part of the design, development, and evaluation of instructional materials. Carr and Datiles (1980) present a two-stage model for the design and development of materials and their systematic assessment and appraisal. In a mental health setting, the coordinator and the staff development committee can establish professional growth teams that function much like the peer review groups described by Carr and Datiles. These teams are important in that they help individuals establish their own goals and projects in an atmosphere that is conducive to professional growth. Staff growth and improvement should always be foremost among the goals of any professional development plan, and instructional materials should be developed to achieve measurable objectives that are part of these overall goals. It is only in this context that the success of these materials can be adequately judged.

At the center, growth teams were composed of designated members of the staff development committee who worked with selected professionals from the community and the region. Staff members from the development committee chose these professionals as advisers. Staff and advisers worked together to develop curriculum, set standards of evaluation, and attract qualified credentialed resource people as trainers. Curriculum units and learning objectives were developed in such areas as psychopharmacology and aging, long-term care administration, rural psychology and isolation-depression, middle-aged offspring of elderly parents, chemical dependency and the aged, and psychoanalysis and the aged. The staff developed pretest and posttest evaluation procedures, while the teams developed action plans for each curriculum unit in order to establish public relations programming, training schedules, resource people, evaluation procedures, and locations.

Meaningful Verbal Material

Much of the information on audiotapes and videotapes is verbal. The use of an interactional rhetoric, which is concerned with act, scene, agency, and purpose, is therefore important (McMeen, 1982). Given Gagné's view (Gagné and Wiegand, 1970) that propositions rather than individual words are stored in long-term memory, it is also necessary to consider a cognitive strategy, such as a theory of meaningful reception learning, to explain the meaningful form of these propositions and their assimilation (McMeen, 1983). The subsumption of meaningful verbal materials into cognitive structure and the role of advance organizers is presented as a theory of meaningful reception learning by Ausubel (1968). A strategy for developing advance organizers and for using rhetorical sentences that help anchor ideas in memory is advocated by McMeen (1983). Such a strategy is particularly relevant to the development of audiovisual materials in which verbal messages are dominant.

Rhetorical development of a script for an audiotape or a videotape may follow from a consideration of the rhetorical elements of Burke's (1969) interactional pentad, while meaningful development may be based upon Gagné and Wiegand's (1970) descriptions of context sequences. Not all audiotapes and videotapes will need to be produced with this attention to development. Some will lack this kind of development because they are spontaneous recordings of speakers and other activities. Recordings such as these, however, will fulfill a purpose as instructional resources in that they offer a transcription of the ideas and thoughts of guest speakers as well as a description of the content of meetings and seminars. These recordings will generally lack development according to an instructional strategy unless speakers have some strategy in mind, and they will not have been developed through the use of a script, which is perhaps more amenable to a development that uses instructional strategy. Nevertheless, wherever the development of instructional materials is contemplated, concern for meaningful verbal learning and an interactional rhetoric will be helpful in developing a suitable context for the meaningful propositions that are frequently encountered in communication.

At the center, the development staff focused on important concepts related to the training units. The staff used these concepts within the context of continuous verbal interactions. In the area of aging, it was useful to use a concept-based, script-oriented learning strategy. One such strategy focused on the organizing concept of "myths of aging." In this strategy, a videotape produced by the staff featured a psychoanalyst who addressed principal myths of aging. In other cases, staff videotaped lectures and discussions designed for long-term use. The staff often scheduled follow-up sessions in order to underline important concepts.

The staff always focused on a planned rhetorical strategy and key concepts that could be used in an interaction model. One example of this is the audiovisual production that emphasized the myths of aging. Another example was the curriculum unit titled "Middle-Aged Children of Elderly Parents." This idea proved to be a valuable organizing concept and basis for a variety of interactive modes, including interactions among middle-aged offspring, about common problems. Additionally, the staff used audiovisuals that focused on intergenerational role playing and served as the basis for discussion among middle-aged offspring.

Conclusion

In the experience of the Southeast Mental Health Center, a staff development model that has three separate tracks for professional growth has helped improve individual staff qualifications as well as the agency's relationships with other institutions and with the community. Audiotapes and videotapes were used to advantage in the implementation of individually negotiated career development goals, in-service training, and continuing education. Their use with adults in continuing education and at other educational levels is supported by research.

In this application, audiotapes and videotapes were used both as instructional resources and as instructional components for the three professional development tracks. As an instructional method, Audio-Assisted Independent Study holds promise for many areas of continuing education, including the mental health field, as a means of providing formal instruction to adults. Moreover, professional growth teams are important to the attainment of staff development when they function in a setting where individual career development goals are negotiated and peer review is an essential part of the design, development, and evaluation of instructional materials.

It is apparent that the instructional design of audiotapes and videotapes should employ some instructional strategy for the development of these materials. To the extent that much information may be verbal and may contain meaningful propositions, a strategy that relates meaningful learning by using advance organizers and an interactional rhetoric should be considered in staff development.

Finally, the mental health field is similar to other areas of continuing education in that it looks to a model for developing staff and to instructional media as a means of communicating instructional information for the attainment of a professional development program.

References

Ausubel, D. P. *Educational Psychology: A Cognitive View.* New York: Holt, Rinehart & Winston, 1968.

Berger, E. J. "An Investigation of the Effectiveness of Televised Presentations of Self-Contained Television Adapted Lessons on Enrichment Topics in Mathematics." *Dissertation Abstracts,* 1962, *23,* 1552.

Bickel, R. F. "A Comparative Analysis of the Effect of Television on Achievement in a College Mathematics Course for Elementary Teaching Majors." *Dissertation Abstracts,* 1965, *25,* 5777.

Burke, K. *A Grammar of Motives.* Berkeley: University of California Press, 1969.

Burke, W. W. *Organizational Development: Principals and Practices.* Boston: Little, Brown, 1982.

Carr, V. H., Jr., and Datiles, U. P. "Systematic Assessment and Appraisal of Instructional Materials." *Technological Horizons in Education Journal,* 1980, *7* (1), 51–52.

Educational Technology. Interview with Robert M. Gagné, June 1982, 11–15.

Gagné, R. M., and Wiegand, V. K. "Effects of a Superordinate Context on Learning and Retention of Facts." *Journal of Educational Psychology,* 1970, *61* (5), 406–409.

Klapper, H. L. *Closed Circuit Television as a Medium of Instruction at New York University 1956–1957.* New York: New York University, 1958.

Lippitt, G. L. *Organizational Renewal: A Holistic Approach to Organization Development.* Englewood Cliffs, N.J.: Prentice-Hall, 1982.

McMeen, G. R. "In Search of Mediator and Rhetoric: Toward a Strategy for Communicating Verbal Information in Multimedia Instructional Materials." *Educational Technology,* 1982, *22* (2), 9–12.

McMeen, G. R. "Toward the Development of Rhetoric and Context in the Communication of Meaningful Verbal Information in Multimedia Instructional Materials." *Educational Technology,* 1983 (in press).

Menne, J. W., Klingensmith, J. E., and Nord, N. D. "The Feasibility of Using Taped Lectures to Replace Class Attendance." Paper presented at the American Educational Research Association, Los Angeles, 1969. (ED 027 748)

Pollack, T. C., Cargill, O., Loomis, J., and Zarbaugh, H. *Closed-Circuit Television as a Medium of Instruction 1955–1958.* New York: New York University, 1956.

Popham, W. J. "Tape Recorded Lectures in the College Classroom." *AV Communication Review,* 1961, *9,* 109–118.

Stanley, J., and Reich, P. "Teaching Blood Morphology: Audiovisual Method Compared to Microscope Slides with Written Text and Instructor." *Blood,* 1974, *44,* 445–448.

Thorman, J. H. "The Video Tape Presentation Versus the 'Live' Presentation: Better, Worse or the Same?" *Technological Horizons in Education Journal,* 1974, *1* (4), 24–27.

Thorman, J. H. "Continuing Education for Adults Utilizing Videotape as an Instructional Component." *T.H.E. Journal,* 1975, *2* (8), 21–22, 30.

Thorman, J. H. "Continuing Education for Adults Utilizing Audiotape Cassettes as an Instructional Component." *Association for Continuing Higher Education Region X Newsletter,* 1976, *1* (2), 1–3.

Thorman, J. H., and Amb, T. "Videotape/Discussion—Lecture/Discussion: A Comparison." *Educational and Industrial Television,* 1972, *4* (11), 26, 29–31.

Wasson, J. B., and Thorman, J. H. *Instruction with Tape Cassettes.* Technical Report No. 1, Department of Education, Moorhead State University, Moorhead, Minnesota, 1975.

Peter Geib teaches management at Moorhead State University, Moorhead, Minnesota, where he is assistant professor in the Department of Business Administration.

George R. McMeen is associate professor and coordinator of audiovisual and television at Moorhead State University. He has taught several courses in media education using the Audio-Assisted Independent Study method, and he is the author of numerous articles about rhetoric and the use of context in multimedia instructional materials.

A flexible, versatile teaching tool, slide sets can be an effective and creative part of teaching with attention to a few basic principles.

Slide Sets: Development and Selection for Use in Teaching Adults

David J. Miller

Slides are always popular as a teaching tool. Because of their versatility, they can be an effective device if used appropriately but can detract from learning objectives if they are not. In selecting slides or developing slide sets, it is important to keep some basic principles in mind in order to improve the use of this instructional treasure.

Learning Considerations When Using Slides with Adults

Adults learn best when presented with single concepts in a logical order (Cross, 1976). Slides facilitate learning because most people are visually oriented. Perception of communication is most often in the form of pictures whether the message is verbal or graphic. A word usually carries with it a visual meaning (Lanz, 1980). The words "cat" or "dog" create visual images in the mind; the term "city" carries with it a different visual image than "small town."

During the 1960s and 1970s, when the use of slide sets was increasing, many assessments were made of user preference for, or attitudes toward, various media, patterns of media use, and characteristics of the postsecondary

J. P. Wilson (Ed.). *Materials for Teaching Adults: Selection, Development, and Use.* New Directions for Continuing Education, no. 17. San Francisco: Jossey-Bass, March 1983.

audience. But there are few conclusions reached about the effectiveness of slides as an instructional medium.

According to Campeau (1974), who reviewed the research conducted from 1966 to 1971, no suitable studies were found in which instructional effectiveness of slides, filmstrips, overhead transparencies, or still pictures were assessed. Campeau reports two studies in which slides and filmstrips were used in combination with other media.

When college students with previous business machine experience were taught business machine skills through continuous loop film and slides with tapes, these students learned significantly more than students in a control group taught in the traditional manner. When scores of students with no previous exposure to business machines were analyzed separately, an even greater difference was noted.

Likewise, evaluation of a typing course that used slides with tapes, continuous loop film, and tape recordings showed that students in this experimental situation significantly outperformed the traditionally trained group.

Trohanis (1975) studied the simultaneous projection of multiple slide images with audiotapes as a teaching tool and compared it with conventional methods of instruction. A shorter program length resulted in short-term retention. Test scores were significantly higher for students who viewed slides than for the control group. Short-term retention scores seemed to favor ten-minute slide sets as opposed to twenty-minute or longer slide sets.

Moldstad (1974), who reviewed studies of the integration of various new media into traditional instruction, cites studies of fifth- through seventh-grade children who were exposed to a systems concept of integrating motion pictures and slides. The children showed significantly higher gains in vocabulary as a result of the inclusion of these media.

Moldstad also reviewed a number of studies where audio-tutorial programs in college courses were shown to be superior to conventionally taught courses. Moldstad points out, however, that interest in evaluating the effectiveness of such programs has not paralleled interest in developing them.

While more research is needed, the value of integrating media use with conventional instruction is demonstrated. While it is difficult to assess the exact results of using slides or slide-tape combinations to supplement conventional instruction, it appears that a systems approach, where attention is given to use of such media as a part of total instruction, can be valuable for teaching adults.

Principles of Selecting or Producing Slide Sets

Whether producing slide sets or selecting existing slide sets to meet teaching needs, the same basic principles of planning, production, and use apply. Effective planning can simplify production and use of slide sets. The quality of planning will be reflected in the quality of the completed slide set.

Planning Considerations. Slide sets should have a purpose. It is easy to cover too much in one slide presentation; establish one or two objectives and do a good job of accomplishing those. The task of any visual media is to express an idea or communicate a concept, not to impress with the amount of information available on a subject (Lanz, 1980). While there are no hard and fast rules of what can or cannot be included in slides, the strengths of the medium provide some suggestions.

Paulo Freire (1973) used slides as a means of projecting familiar situations to increase rural Brazilians' consciousness of reality as a prelude to teaching them to read and write. His statement about the role of education in such a situation may be valuable for anyone engaged in continuing education. "The important thing is to help men (and nations) help themselves, to place them in consciously critical confrontation with their problems, to make them agents of their own recuperation" (p. 16).

Because the advantages of slides are ease of sequencing, the ability to show movement and detail, and the capability of bringing inaccessible, indescribable, or irretrievable scenes to the learning group, the most desirable subjects for slides would seem to be subjects where these advantages could be most useful.

In technical training, picture series can be of great value for instruction about assembly methods and processes. Slides can make use of exploded views of objects. By laying out each part adjacent to, but apart from, its related part, viewers can see how bits and pieces fit together. Slides can allow the teacher to bring macrophotography (extreme closeups) to the screen, where the learner can view detail. Superimposing the image of one subject within or beside or over another can be used to show how two items relate to each other.

Slide sets can combine both real scenes and art work to establish continuity and explain relations.

As Langford (1973) says, "Almost unlimited sources of material (are available). Millions of 5 × 5 cm slides are available from producers and libraries covering an ever growing range of subjects. Anything that can be photographed by the teacher or by the students can easily be made into a color slide" (p. 18).

In developing a slide set, always write the script first. There may be debate about which came first, the chicken or the egg, but in quality slide set production, there is little doubt that the script comes first.

Use slides to present new information or to supplement verbal presentations. Plan for handouts to support the points in the slide set since learners cannot take a slide set with them for future reference.

Define the educational objectives at the outset. What should the learner know or be able to do as a result of viewing the slide set? Describe audience characteristics that may affect presentation of the information (such as age, interests, and present knowledge of the subject). Describe the relation of the subject matter to the need of the audience. Reconsider the various media. Are slides really the best media for teaching this concept?

If a slide set is in order, develop an outline. Identify the concept to be taught, and then list the facets of the concept in the order needed for understanding the concept. Gather material and information pertaining to the various facets of the concept.

Write the script as though talking conversationally to each person in the audience. Use short sentences and simple words. Simple, short words have more punch than long words.

Try to get the audience's attention with the first sentence or two. Let the narrative flow like a story, and the slides can be planned to coincide with and visualize the story.

Be sincere; use the present tense as much as possible. Give the listener a signal when moving from one subject to another by using transitional phrases. Avoid tongue-twisting words or phrases. Remember, someone is going to have to narrate the script. Write numbers out and do not use abbreviations.

Production. There are many facets of producing a slide set for discussion. There are also some excellent references available to help you with production (Fisher, 1980; Peck, n.d.). For the purposes of this chapter, general principles of slide production will be discussed. Details of production will be left to more specialized publications.

Once a script is written, production cards may be useful in illustrating it (Billings, 1980). The idea in developing a slide set is to present ideas visually and to use the words of the script as a supplement. The production card should help achieve a happy blend of the verbal and the visual.

Go through the script using production cards and identify each point that should be made. For each point, think how it can be shown in picture form. Sketching stick figures or rough illustrations on the card may be useful. Describe the illustration on the card and the commentary it pictures. Decide if the visual idea is best presented as a photograph, a sketch or drawing, or by writing it out. List this under the heading "production notes."

If production cards do not seem feasible, type the script at the right side of a piece of paper and leave room at the left margin for sketching or describing the visualization of the commentary.

Consider existing slides and decide which slides are still needed. When deciding how many slides will be needed to visualize the script, plan for a minimum of six to seven seconds for the fastest slide change. Usually, a maximum of fifteen seconds can be allowed to keep a slide on the screen in a slide set accompanied by an audio tape narration.

There are many good sources of detailed information on actually taking the photographs, and several on producing charts, graphs, and title slides (Langford, 1973; Fisher, 1980; Breneman, n.d.). There are some general principles to keep in mind when illustrating the script.

Generally, it is best to use only horizontal slides. Vertical slides often reach above and below the lighted area of the normal screen when it is set for horizontal slides. Alternating between vertical and horizontal slides in the same set tends to create a hodge-podge effect, affects the smooth flow of the slide story, and may distract the viewers.

In general, pictures should be kept simple, with the center of interest being the most important single element of the picture. Usually, the eyes of the viewer will be drawn toward the lightest area in a photograph. Placing the center of interest in the center of the picture may not make the most interesting composition. Mentally divide the camera viewfinder into thirds, using both vertical and horizontal lines, and compose the picture so the center of interest falls where two of these lines cross. The picture usually will be more interesting than if it was centered.

Create a feeling of depth by a technique called framing. Framing means composing a picture with an object (such as a tree branch or a group of people) closer to the camera than is the center of interest.

Try to shoot active pictures with the people in them doing something. Take the photograph at the most dramatic or timely moment. Plan for the pictures needed; give directions, and tell the subjects what to do. Candid shots are seldom satisfactory, and may not achieve exactly what is required. Low camera angles tend to imply strength, while higher camera angles will tend to make the subject appear less dramatic.

When the slides are collected, put the slides in sequence on a lighttable or slidesorter, or in a projector where they can be seen readily. Read the script out loud and follow along with the slides. Some final questions about the slides and script may be useful at this stage.

1. Does the slide contribute to the objectives of the slide set?
2. Does the slide focus attention on one main idea?
3. Have all of the nonessential elements been taken away from the picture, leaving the main idea intact?
4. How does the commentary fit the slides? Do changes need to be made in the commentary?
5. Are the title slides legible and short enough to be read easily?

If audio is to be added to the slide set, consider having someone else help record the narration. Alternating voices helps give the viewers more variety. Often, audio tape narration accompanying the slide set can give added flexibility in using the slide set. It can guarantee a satisfactory narration (in fact, a uniform narration) with a professional voice no matter who shows the slide set. Using a taped narration is easier than trying to follow a script while holding a flashlight, changing slides at the proper time, and attempting to narrate. If there is an inaudible electronic signal on the tape to change slides automatically, the slide set can flow smoothly, while audible beeps may disconcern or irritate the viewer.

If the narration is to be recorded, it is more convenient for the person showing the slides if a description of the slide that is to appear on the screen is included to the left of the corresponding commentary on the script. If the description is included, someone can change slides manually without the necessity of putting an audible beep on the tape.

Adding audio can also allow music to be added to set a mood for the presentation and make listening easier.

Accompanying the slide set with an audio tape poses some technical problems for producer and user. For the user, it means a synchronized tape recorder and projector unit must be available. For the producer, it means arranging for the use of production equipment that can mix music and narration or other sounds.

There are portable self-contained projectors, tape recorders, and screen units that allow showing of slides and tape playing. By pushing a button, an electronic signal to change slides can be added to the tape rather easily. There are also tape recorder units on the market that allow synchronization with a projector unit that can be used to add the electronic signal to the tape. Using these units, tapes can be produced with narration and electronic signals, and perhaps musical background, with relative ease. If the tape is produced separately, the instructor can use this equipment to add the inaudible signals for changing slides. If signals are placed on the tape by the teacher, a copy of the tape (not the master) should be used just in case a mistake is made. If there is time available to experiment with this sort of equipment, it is possible to be quite creative and develop well-produced, effective slide sets.

Use of Slide Sets

The way in which the viewer is exposed to the slide set is as important as planning and production considerations. The audience must be able to see and understand the visual presentation easily. The audience needs to feel good about the authority of the information contained in the slide set.

Choose a screen that is adequate for the audience. According to Dossin (1971), the width of the screen should be approximately one-sixth the distance from the screen to the back row.

Use a black slide, or a two-inch square piece of hard plastic made for the purpose, or a square of thin cardboard at the beginning and ending of your slides to avoid blank spaces and brilliant flashes of projector light. Using a blank slide allows the projector to be turned on ahead of time without distracting from the presentation. Learn to feel comfortable in operating the projection equipment. Practice, preview, and show the slides at least once before presenting them to the intended viewers.

Planning, developing, and using slide sets can be creative and rewarding. Slides can assist effectively in teaching. A few basic principles of planning, production, and use can provide the tools needed to develop or select and use slide sets effectively.

References

Billings, T. E. "Planning a Slide Presentation." Unpublished paper, College of Agriculture, University of Missouri, 1980.

Breneman, D. *Making Your Point with Pictures*. (Department of Information Series No. 14.) St. Paul, Minn.: University of Minnesota, n.d.

Campeau, P. L. "Selective Review of the Results of Research on the Use of Audiovisual Media to Teach Adults." *Audio-Visual Communications Review*, 1974, *22* (1), 5–40.

Cross, K. P. *Accent on Learning*. San Francisco: Jossey-Bass, 1976.

Dossin, C., Jr. *Projector Tips for Carousel and Ektagraphic Projectors*. University Park: Pennsylvania State University, 1971.

Fisher, H. L. *Making Effective Slides for Meetings*. Berkeley: University of California Division of Agricultural Sciences, 1980.

Freire, P. *Education for Critical Consciousness*. New York: Seabury, 1973.

Langford, M. *Visual Aids and Photography in Education*. New York: Hastings House, 1973.

Lanz, M. *The Power of a Visual*. Fargo: North Dakota Cooperative Extension Service, 1980.

Moldstad, J. A. "Selective Review of Research Studies Showing Media Effectiveness: A Primer for Media Directors. *Audio-Visual Communications Review*, 1974, *22* (4), 387–407.

Peck, E. G. *Twenty Minute Color Slide Recipe*. Manhattan, Kan.: Cooperative Extension Service, n.d.

Trohanis, P. L. "Information Learning and Retention with Multiple-Images and Audio." *AV Communications Review*, 1975, *23* (4), 395–414.

David J. Miller is associate professor in international agricultural programs at the University of Missouri and a consultant working with Cooperative Extension communications and training systems. He has over twenty years of experience in Cooperative Extension training and communications in Missouri, North Dakota, and Iowa.

There is no best medium for producing attitudinal outcomes,
but there is probably a best approach for maximizing desirable
outcomes in a specific situation.

Designing Instructional Media for Attitudinal Outcomes

Michael R. Simonson

As early as 1931, Thurstone was able to demonstrate the impact of film on attitudes. In this landmark study it was found that two films, one depicting the Chinese favorably, the other unfavorably, were capable of producing either positive or negative changes in attitude. While this type of study would be socially unacceptable today, it did demonstrate that media could be used to change attitudes.

Since Thurstone's study, numerous experiments have evaluated some aspect of the relationship between instructional media and attitude formation and attitude change in learners. Over 200 of these experiments were reviewd by Simonson (1980). Generally, the result of those studies are not uniform enough to produce a single, definitive conclusion concerning the relationship between mediated instruction and attitudes. Results are often contradictory. However, there are many studies in which researchers reported findings where instructional media were used to deliver messages and desired or hypothesized attitudinal outcomes resulted.

While a review of the literature is not intended here, it is important for those interested in designing persuasive messages to be aware of the type and scope of positive relationship that reportedly exists between mediated instruction and the attitudes of learners. This chapter documents procedures that were successful in experimental situations in producing desired attitudinal

J. P. Wilson (Ed.). *Materials for Teaching Adults: Selection, Development, and Use.* New Directions for Continuing Education, no. 17. San Francisco: Jossey-Bass, March 1983.

outcomes. These techniques are supported by citing a sample of specific research studies where the procedure was successfully validated. Many of these studies were based on settings different than most in continuing education and involved considerably younger subjects. Therefore, one should apply these recommendations skeptically. The nature of educational research prohibits the development of conclusions about the learning process than can be universally applied. The following statements are intended as guidelines only, not laws or rules.

Design Guidelines

Once it is decided that a certain attitude change is desirable, there are some procedures that can promote certain attitudinal outcomes in learners. The six guidelines listed below are intended as recommendations to consider during the design of instruction.

Guideline 1. Learners seem to react favorably to mediated instruction that is realistic, relevant to them, and technically stimulating. Levonian (1963) reported on a preproduction survey of the target audience in order to ascertain their attitudinal positions (among other things) about India. The results of this study were used in the production of a persuasive film on India. Supposedly, this approach made the resulting instruction more relevant and realistic to the audience, and this contributed to attitude changes. Tests of this hypothesis indicated that desired attitude positions were produced in viewers of the film.

Seiler (1971) found that persuasive messages presented by media were most effective if the visual channel supplemented the verbal through the use of technically relevant graphics or good quality human interest photographs. Klapper (1958) also reported that highly visualized lessons were perceived as most realistic by learners, and seemed most likely to produce desired attitudes.

Relevance and realism were examined further by Croft and others (1969) and Donaldson (1976). Both reported that "live" messages were the most realistic to learners and were most effective in producing attitude changes toward intercollegiate athletics and the disabled. Television messages on these topics were found to be next most realistic and effective. Booth and Miller (1974) investigated the realism provided by pictures produced in color versus those in black and white. They reported a relationship between the use of color, realism, and attitude formation.

Two additional studies provided interesting information on the correlation between realism and attitude change. McFarlane (1945) found that subjects seemed most influenced attitudinally by story films rather than non-story films. Ganschow and others (1970) also reported nonstatistically significant, but important, trends in a study on attitudes toward occupations. It was found that when an actor's ethnic group was the same as a viewer's, the subject identified with the actor, thought the instruction was realistic, and scored higher on attitude-toward-actor's-occupation inventories.

While this sample of studies certainly provides far from conclusive support for Guideline One, it does seem evidence enough to warrant consideration of this idea when specific attitude outcomes are desired.

Guideline Two. *Learners seem to be persuaded, and react favorably, when mediated instruction includes the presentation of new information about the topic.* Levonian's (1963) studies lend support to the intent of this guideline. When the audience was surveyed about India, it was possible for the developer of the film to use this information to ascertain previous knowledge about India so that new information could be presented. This new information was included to support the attitude position desired by Levonian. Jouko (1972) reported similar results. It was found that the less preinstruction knowledge students had about a topic, the more attitude change was produced after an informational and persuasive lesson. In other words, there was a negative relationship between preinstruction familiarity with the topic and attitude change as a result of a persuasive communication.

A similar conclusion was proposed by Knowlton and Hawes (1962). They correlated attitude with knowledge about a topic and found a positive relationship. In this study it was determined that knowledge about a topic was often a necessary prerequisite for a learner to have a positive attitude position toward the idea. Stated another way, new knowledge may need to be supplied when attitude changes are desired, or knowledge may need to be present for a learner to have a favorable attitude toward a topic.

A corollary to Guideline Two was proposed by Peterson and Thurstone (1933). They reported that young viewers were influenced more by persuasive films than were older ones. They also found that a series of related films seemed to produce a cumulative influence on attitudes. Possibly, younger subjects acquired more new information than older, more knowledgeable ones as a result of viewing the persuasive films, and this contributed to significantly greater attitude changes.

It would seem that positive attitudinal outcomes are more likely to occur when the cognitive components of attitude are considered in the design of persuasive instruction. Level of knowledge is an important variable when attitudinal outcomes are sought.

Guideline Three. *Learners seem positively affected when persuasive messages are presented in as credible a manner as possible.* Source credibility has been recognized as an important criteria for attitude change since the early 1950s. When mediated instruction is developed it will often be valued positively, and attitudinal positions advocated in the materials will be influential if the persuasive message is delivered by a credible source or in a credible way. Kishler (1950) found that when the actor in a persuasive film was cast as a member of a highly credible occupational group, it was likely that attitude changes advocated by the actor would occur.

Credibility can also be simulated by the way material is presented. Seiler (1971) produced three videotaped versions of a persuasive speech on the

Vietnam War. It was found that the greatest amounts of attitude change were produced in learners who viewed either technical graphics or human interest photographs as a part of their visual message as contrasted to a talking-free version. It was concluded that the visuals added credibility to the persuasive argument presented in the speech.

O'Brien (1973) provided additional support for Guideline Three in a study dealing with the impact of televised instruction on attitude change. It was found that urban learners identified with television as a method of instruction. Those with a rural background considered live communication to be most credible. In each case, the most credible form of instruction delivered the most powerful attitude change message.

The content of mediated instruction is probably the most critical variable in attitude formation and change. If that information is presented logically and intelligently (in other words, credibly), it is likely that it will be favorably received and will be persuasive.

Guideline Four. *Learners who are involved in the planning, production, or delivery of mediated instruction seem likely to react favorably to the instructional activity and to the message delivered.* Active involvement in the learning process was examined as a component of several research studies. Erickson (1956) found that students who actually produced a film on science concepts reacted more favorably toward instruction and toward science than did students who only watched science films. Coldevin (1975) involved students in message delivery through the use of various review and summarization techniques that were a part of the instructional sequence. It was found that short reviews after television lesson subunits produced the most favorable attitude reports in students. Simonson (1977) conducted an experiment in which adults were enlisted to make counterattitudinal videotapes without realizing that attitude change was the primary purpose of this activity. The process of involving subjects in the making of these videotapes was found to be successful in producing significant attitude changes.

Microteaching is an involvement technique that many educators have found to be successful in changing attitudes of preservice teachers. One study (of many in the literature) that evaluated the impact of microteaching in a somewhat controlled situation was conducted by Goldman (1969). He reported that microteaching produced significant attitude changes in self image in adults.

In the affective domain, the active learner perceives instruction and information more favorably than does the passive learner, all other things being equal. Involvement is an important technique for promoting desirable attitudinal outcomes.

Guideline Five. *Learners who participate in postinstruction discussions and critiques seem likely to develop favorable attitudes toward delivery method and content.* A powerful technique for promoting favorable attitudes has been evaluated by several researchers and consists of the addition of follow-up discussions to the instructional sequence. These follow-ups usually involve learners in an analysis or critique of the instruction and message presented. Allison (1966) found that only when postviewing discussions were included after students had watched motivational science films did significant attitude change occur. Fay (1974) reported similar findings in a study that used follow-up activities for a film on the problems of the handicapped and the need for barrier-free buildings. Attitudes toward continuing education were significantly altered after classroom teachers saw a film and participated in a discussion on the subject (Burrichter, 1968).

An interesting variation on the studies previously reported was conducted by Domyahn (1972). In this experiment, adults viewed a nonpersuasive film on the responsibility for the fall of eastern Europe to the communists after World War II. Domyahn reported that attitude changes were produced only in the treatment groups that participated in persuasive critiques after viewing the film.

Guidelines Three and Four are directed toward the behavioral component of attitude. When learners are involved in the instructional situation, it is likely that they will value the learning process positively and will maintain or develop favorable attitudes toward the content presented.

Guideline Six. *Learners who experience a purposeful emotional involvement or arousal during instruction are likely to have their attitudes changed in the direction advocated as the purpose of the mediated message.* Janis and Feshbach (1953) presented a slide-audiotape program on the effects of poor dental hygiene to randomly selected young adults. They varied the intensity of a fear-arousing appeal in three versions of the presentation in order to ascertain the most influential delivery technique. All three methods were successful in producing aroused, affective reactions in the students. However, it was found that a minimal fear-arousing appeal was most successful in modifying attitudes because the stronger versions left students in a state of tension that was not alleviated by remedies offered during an accompanying slide show. Janis and Feshbach concluded that strong, fear-producing appeals were not as effective in changing attitudes as were more moderate appeals since the audience was motivated to ignore the importance of the threat in order to reduce the tension they felt.

Rogers (1973) reported on a study that supported this position. Public health films dealing with cigarette smoking, safe driving, and venereal disease were tested in three different studies. It was found that the more noxious a film was, the more fear that was aroused in viewers. However, it was also reported that these fear-arousing films were most effective in changing attitudes when preventatives or statements of probability of exposure to the malady discussed in the film were included as part of the motion picture.

Miller (1969) examined the degree of emotional involvement produced in viewers of motion or still picture versions of the same script. It was reported that the motion picture version produced a higher positive evaluation by students. Miller concluded that this was due to the increased intellectual involvement in viewers of motion pictures.

Again, the studies supporting Guideline Six indicate that viewers' participation in the learning process is important when attitudinal outcomes are desired. In these cases, involvement was emotional rather than behavioral, as it was in the studies cited to support Guidelines Four and Five. Learner involvement is a powerful technique for the continuing educator to use if attitudinal outcomes are to be an important consequence of instruction.

Conclusion

Attitudinal outcomes should be of concern to the developer of teaching materials. Techniques likely to produce a favorable reaction in students should be routinely identified, refined, and evaluated as a part of the design and delivery of instruction. It is readily apparent after studying the foregoing guidelines and research that media is only one influence on attitudes. Media is primarily a carrier of information in these studies. There is no best medium for producing attitudinal outcomes. However, there is probably a best approach for the development of instruction that will maximize desirable attitudes in a specific situation. By critically applying the general guidelines listed above, the continuing educator should be well on the way to influencing attitude change.

References

Allison, R. W. "The Effect of Three Methods of Teaching Motivational Films upon Attitudes of Fourth, Fifth, and Sixth Grade Students Toward Science, Scientists, and Scientific Careers." Unpublished doctoral dissertation, Pennsylvania State University, 1966. *Dissertation Abstracts,* 1966, *28,* 994.

Booth, G. D., and Miller, H. R. "Effectiveness of Monochrome and Color Presentations Facilitating Affective Learning." *AV Communication Review,* 1974, *22,* 409–422.

Burrichter, A. W. "A Study of Elementary Public School Personnel Attitudes Toward Continuing Education in Selected Communities in Wyoming: An Experiment in Changing Adult Attitudes and Concepts." Unpublished doctoral dissertation, University of Wyoming, 1968.

Coldevin, G. O. "Spaced, Massed, and Summary as Review Strategies for ITV Production." *AV Communication Review,* 1975, *23,* 289–303.

Croft, R. G., Stimpson, D. V., Ross, W. L., Bray, R. M., and Breglio, V. J. "Comparison of Attitude Changes Elicited by Live and Videotape Classroom Presentations."*AV Communication Review,* 1969, *17,* 315–321.

Domyahn, R. A. "The Effects of a Non-Persuasive Film, a Specially Designed Persuasive Critique, and a Non-Persuasive Group Discussion on Attitude and Retention of Information." Unpublished doctoral dissertation, University of Iowa, 1972. *Dissertation Abstracts International,* 1973, *33,* 6586A.

Donaldson, J. "Channel Variations and Effects on Attitudes Toward Physically Disabled Individuals." *AV Communication Review,* 1976, *24,* 135–144.

Erickson, C. W. H. "Teaching General Science Through Film Production." *AV Communication Review,* 1956, *4,* 268–278.

Fay, F. A. "Effects of a Film, a Discussion Group, and a Role Playing Experience on Architecture Students' Attitudes, Behavioral Intentions, and Actual Behavior Toward Barrier Free Design." Unpublished doctoral dissertation, University of Illinois, 1974. *Dissertation Abstracts International,* 1974, *34,* 6445A.

Ganschow, L. H., Stillwell, W. E., III, and Jones, G. E. *Stimulating Educational Information Seeking and Changes in Student Attitude Toward Vocational Education by Videotape and Film Presentations.* Palo Alto, Calif.: American Institute for Research in the Behavioral Sciences, 1970. (ERIC Document Reproduction Services No. ED 043 778)

Goldman, B. A. *Effect of Classroom Experience and Video Tape Self-Observation Upon Undergraduate Attitudes Toward Self and Toward Teaching.* Washington, D.C.: American Psychological Association, 1969.

Janis, I. L., and Feshbach, S. "Effects of Fear-Arousing Communications." *Journal of Abnormal and Social Psychology,* 1953, *48,* 78–92.

Jouko, C. *The Effect of Directive Teaching Materials on the Affective Learning of Pupils.* Jyvaskyla, Finland: Institute for Educational Research, Report Number 139, 1972.

Kishler, J. P. *The Effects of Prestige and Identification Factors on Attitude Restructuring and Learning from Sound Films.* University Park: Pennsylvania State University, 1950. (ERIC Document Reproduction Service No. ED 053 568)

Klapper, H. L. *Closed-Circuit Television as a Medium of Instruction at New York University, 1956-1957.* A report on New York University's second year of experimentation with television in college classrooms, New York University, 1958.

Knowlton, J., and Hawes, E. "Attitude: Helpful Predictor of Audiovisual Usage?" *AV Communication Review,* 1962, *10,* 147–157.

Levonian, E. "Opinion Change as Mediated by an Audience-Tailored Film." *AV Communication Review,* 1963, *11,* 104–113.

McFarlane, A. M. "A Study of the Influence of an Educational Geographical Film on the Racial Attitudes of a Group of Elementary School Students." *British Journal of Educational Psychology,* 1945, *15,* 152–153.

Miller, W. C. "Film Movement and Affective Response and the Effect on Learning and Attitude Formation." *AV Communication Review,* 1969, *17,* 172–181.

O'Brien, S. J. "The Effect of Television Instruction on Problem Solving Attitudes of Fifth and Sixth Grade Students." Unpublished doctoral dissertation, Oregon State University, 1973. *Dissertation Abstracts International,* 1973, *34,* 2277A

Peterson, R. C., and Thurstone, L. L. *Motion Pictures and the Social Attitudes of Children.* New York: Macmillan, 1933.

Rogers, R. W. *An Analysis of Fear Appeals and Attitude Change.* Final report, Grant No. 1 Roe MH22157-01 MSM, National Institute of Mental Health, University of South Carolina, Chapel Hill, 1973.

Seiler, W. "The Effects of Visual Materials on Attitudes, Credibility, and Retention." *Speech Monographs,* 1971, *38,* 331–334.

Simonson, M. R. "Attitude Change and Achievement: Dissonance Theory in Education." *Journal of Education Research,* 1977, *70* (3), 163–169.

Simonson, M. R. "Media and Attitudes: An Annotated Bibliography of Selected Research—Part II." *Educational Communication and Technology Journal,* 1980, *28* (1), 47–61.

Thurstone, L. L. "Influence of Motion Pictures on Children's Attitudes." *Journal of Social Psychology,* 1931, *2,* 232–234.

Michael R. Simonson is professor of secondary education at Iowa State University and is president of the research and theory division of the Association for Educational Communication and Technology. His research, publication, and teaching interests center on curriculum and instructional media.

When powerless groups create materials for their own learning, they may learn to create their own history and thus challenge those who oppress them.

Material for Learning and Acting: Video and Social Change

Thomas W. Heaney

Most enterprises in the United States are judged by their outcomes—the results or products they produce. Such judgments are an expression of a long-dominant American philosophy: pragmatic functionalism. Most of us have, as part of the philosophical lens through which we view the world, a product orientation. We accept a technological model of our world in which reality presents us with multiple problems to be solved and human history is a spiral of progress in the application of methods or techniques toward the elimination of these problems.

Such a model demands experts, usually technicians, who have mastered specialized knowledge that gives them effective control over the processes of social change. In education, this technological model requires behavioral objectives, quantifiable results, and ultimately the commodification of knowledge—the marketing of knowledge in modules and prepackaged materials for mass markets. Commercial and most educational media are well suited to the product orientation of the technological model. They are slick, utilize high-cost technologies, and demand expert technicians. Mass media silence us with their dazzling images and cacophonous sounds and create a passive, television-addicted, homogenized society. Tools for learning take on

J. P. Wilson (Ed.). *Materials for Teaching Adults: Selection, Development, and Use.* New Directions for Continuing Education, no. 17. San Francisco: Jossey-Bass, March 1983.

the configuration of tools for technical production, and we, professional continuing educators, become the essential technicians of a learning society.

How does this model affect those who have the least to gain from products of the technological society — namely, the poor? The poor, who are variously identified as disadvantaged, disenfranchised, culturally or educationally deprived, and illiterate, are always described in terms of needs and deficiencies. And deficiencies, in the technological model, demand services. Needs, of course, are identified by service providers. Thus, continuing educators, as service providers, not only provide the answers, but the questions as well. This is a convenient arrangement!

Problems and Alternatives

Unfortunately, there are many problems with the service economy and the technological model on which it is based. For one, because the employment of a growing number of professional service providers depends on the identification of more and more needs, needs are created at a far greater rate than the services that meet them. Second, the model overlooks a major problem of dependent groups by adding yet one more class of professionals on which the disadvantaged must depend, namely, the service providers. The ultimate consequence of the technological model is too often the unwitting adaptation of dependent and disadvantaged groups to a social order in which they will suffer permanent disadvantage. Such an economy is poorly suited to empowering the poor and uneducated to change their world.

Alternate strategies are demanded by those who share this critique of the technological model. Many continuing educators have rejected the pragmatic functionalism just described and have developed broadly aimed projects in which community and continuing educators collaborate in mutual education. Such projects have few foreseeable behavioral objectives or quantifiable results. They are not product- but, rather, process-oriented. They stress the journey and not the destination. The content of such learning is principally the process; that is, learning is primarily reflected in day-to-day life — action engaged in, oppressions endured, not in linear progression, but with the circular randomness of life itself.

In such an alternate strategy, no expert or technician plans the sequenced events that build a curriculum. Events happen, not by chance or with mindless abandon, but they happen as a result of the unanticipated order imposed by the community itself as the community begins to reflect on and eventually create its own history. Such programs address the issue of empowerment. From the perspective of those who seek to preserve the present social order with its unequal distribution of power, such programs seem ambiguous, ill-defined, and fraught with risk. The risk of such an alternate strategy is real. As in the redistribution of land, those who own the land are at risk of losing it. So also in learning that results in empowerment: Those who have a vested interest in the present economy of power are at risk of losing their advantages. This alternative to the technological model has been called, by some continuing educators, "liberatory education" (Freire, 1970). Liberatory education requires the development of liberatory tools and materials for learning. Given the overall aim of empowerment leading to social change, such tools and materials will be interactive; they will emphasize and incorporate the collective energies of learners who are simultaneously producers and receivers of knowledge and skills, whether these tools are electronic (as with television and computer-assisted learning,) oral (as in dialogue with a teacher or with other learners), or printed materials. The remainder of this chapter is concerned primarily with the interactive use of media, especially television, as a source of learning materials in liberatory education.

Interactive Media for Liberatory Education

Interactive media parallel the development of literacy in Freire's terms. These media provide not only prepackaged words, but a voice. Learners can use video and other media to articulate and visualize their own reality and thus come to know it as well as share it. Because the content of liberatory learning is day-to-day experiences, the materials for such learning must express these experiences. Through the use of video and other recording media, learners are able to document their experiences and thus reflect on and validate them. The emphasis in liberatory media is not on the document, but on documenting—on deciding what is important, whom or what to record, and how to control the use to which the resulting tape will be put (Hopkinson, 1971). After the process is completed, the document is no longer important; materials for such education are disposable and recyclable.

Television is a powerful tool. For learners it can be a voice, rather than a product to be consumed. It is a weapon. A video camera can empower; it can be used as a weapon to intimidate, to influence public policy, to force public accountability, to organize otherwise apathetic individuals into an effective force for social change (Theodore, 1977–1978). Or, as John Ohliger has stated, "The keystone concept of all this work is involvement. Fresh, intense, nonprofessional, open, committed involvement of people who are ordinarily safely labeled and sidetracked as the target audience" (1974, p. 3).

The Fogo Island Project

This use of media for learning related to social change began with Challenge for Change, a unit of the National Film Board of Canada formed in the late 1960s. Fogo Island, ten miles off the northeast coast of Newfoundland, provided a setting for the first project of Challenge for Change. Fewer than five thousand people lived on the island and were divided into small settlements with little communication among them. The decline of inshore fishing on the island had placed 60 percent of the population on welfare. There were no active unions or producer cooperatives. The residents of Fogo were trapped in isolation and poverty and lacked both the knowledge and confidence to escape.

Film crews went to Fogo Island intent on producing several conventional documentary films that could increase the islanders' consciousness of problems and solutions. Instead, a process emerged that involved groups all over the island in screening the raw footage and examining one another's views without direct confrontation or hostility. They began to recognize the commonality of their problems and their identity as Fogo Islanders. The films (twenty-eight short films totaling six hours) were eventually edited to reflect the emerging consensus of the people of the island.

The next and most important problem was how to communicate with the mainland politicians and civil servants who could decide the fate of the island. Two days of screenings were organized and the results were astounding. As one film board official said, "We finally had fishermen talking to cabinet ministers. If you take fishermen to the cabinet, they won't talk about the problems of their lives the way they will among other fishermen. But if you let government people look at films of fishermen talking together, the message comes through" (Gwyn, 1972, p. 6). After the screenings, the comments and responses of several ministers were recorded and played back to Fogo Islanders. Substantial and long-term development resulted from these exchanges: Local self-government was organized, a fishermen's cooperative was formed, and plans were begun for building a new multipurpose fish plant. The problems for the island were now problems of growth and not decline.

This process became known as the Fogo Process and has served as a model for education and social change efforts throughout the world (Hopkins and others, 1972). Most notable among these efforts has been the work of Broadside TV in the Tennessee mountains, the Parallel Institute in Montreal, Metro Media in Vancouver, the Alternate Media Center in New York, Community Video in London, and Communications for Change in Chicago. One recent example of the Fogo Process in continuing education is provided by a project in southwest Rockford, Illinois.

Rockford Interactive Media Project

Southwest Rockford is a 1,466-acre community in Illinois cordoned off from the rest of the city by railroad tracks, cul-de-sacs, the Rock River, and other natural and planned barriers. Its predominant population is black, interspersed with Italians and Latinos. A majority of its residents live in single and two-family substandard housing. The average family income is $9,000. About 30 percent of the families have annual incomes of less than $5,000. Over 50 percent of the minority population has not graduated from high school. Self-determination and effective involvement in decision making are notably absent.

Community organizations abound, but these organizations—under the coopting influence of city agencies that provide most of their operating budgets—frequently fall prey to intraorganizational squabbles, while the larger issues are ignored. Past failures thwart future initiatives, while local government succeeds at its own version of blaming the victim. Residual energy in the community is often self-destructive.

Our initial objective in southwest Rockford was to collaborate with community residents as they altered the current patterns of noncommunication and noncooperation that divided them and served to separate local groups and city government.

Liberatory education requires the appropriation of tools by people who seek to create appropriate learning materials for their own empowerment. Such people seek fundamental skills in political literacy—a capacity for uttering words that are heard in the tribunals of local government. Materials for political literacy can be developed only with the full involvement of the community. In most instances the community can and should produce its own materials for learning. To facilitate this, educators might begin by placing television programming in the hands of the people. The Rockford Interactive Media Project was a collaborative effort involving Communications for Change in Chicago, the University of Wisconsin–Madison, Northern Illinois University, and the people of southwest Rockford. Since its beginnings in July of 1978, the project staff has trained over forty media activists in the use of portable half-inch video equipment. Video technology, usually controlled by the networks and their sponsors, was made available to community groups and individuals in order to give substance to their voices and amplify their voices so that they could influence decisions that affect these individuals' lives and futures. The project staff used, and trained others to use, video tape recorders to create materials that would enhance critical reflection on day-to-day life and, at the same time, foster learning and understanding among others outside the community, especially government officials and persons with power. The task of developing such educational materials became the vehicle for organizing the community and mobilizing it into action toward mutually agreed-upon goals. Television was thus used to help people help themselves.

The medium of television did this in a variety of ways. Initially, it provided an excuse for conversation in the community. A community organizer might have had difficulty engaging passersby on the street in dialogue, despite the relevance of the issues, but with a microphone or a video camera the organizer could provide the passersby with a reason to stop and talk. Invitations to attend a community meeting might have received an apathetic response, but a meeting featuring the taped conversations of those same passersby attracted not only those who were interviewed but also their parents, cousins, and friends. They were going to be on television and already had a vested interest in the meeting. Later, at the meeting itself, the media provided the community with a vehicle for bringing closure to its own deliberations, and thus the process began.

The process continued until the community had developed a recorded statement (documentation) in which it recognized itself. This did not occur at once, but only after long periods of trial and error, editing, and resubmission of the statement to the community for its approval. The final documentation, when accepted by the community, provided the first words in a dialogue with government officials or whoever else was in a position to respond. The preparation of video and audio tapes had aleady facilitated reflection, articulation, and consensus formation within the community. It had provided an organizational base for the community's active role in political decision making and a bridge for communication and collaboration with government and within itself. It had become the voice of an otherwise silent community. Equally important, the documentation itself remained as a tool for the ongoing education of the community — a permanent record of the people's history and a stimulus for future strategies.

The applications of media undertaken by the Rockford Project were varied. One video documentary told the story of an elderly woman who had tried for two years to get the city to remove a diseased elm from her front yard. Most of Rockford now knows her story, and the city took action. When a community improvement project highly valued by the local residents was suddenly denied funding, a video tape recorded the distress of previously unemployed workers, the anger of the community organization that had sponsored the project, and the outrage of the people of the community itself, who had taken such pride in the project's accomplishments. The tape forced a reconsideration of the matter by the local CETA consortium.

Probably the most interesting case study generated during the first year of the project was one involving the state's office for Title I-A of the Higher Education Act, through which funding for the project had been obtained. The initial proposal had specified that the video equipment purchased for the project would remain with the community after the first year. The university agreed to continue providing technical assistance as needed, but its resources would no longer be needed to sustain the project. The community, now trained in the use of interactive media, would continue to use the equipment to develop materials that would raise levels of consciousness concerning local issues and problems.

But as the first year of the project came to an end, the Title I office decided to recall the equipment. Participants in the project were convinced that their successes (and near successes) had led local government to use its influence in the state capital in order to eliminate the project. They decided to use the interactive media process, for which they had been trained with Title I funds, against the Title I office. The state director for Title I funds initially refused to meet with representatives of the black and Hispanic communities in Rockford, but after community members contacted several newly won friends in the state legislature, the meeting was scheduled. The meeting was taped, much to the consternation of the state director, who subsequently feared that the tape could damage his image in the state as an advocate for minority interests. The day after the meeting the state director called one of the leaders of the community and told them they had won; they could keep the equipment. The equipment remained in Rockford for another year, but, equally important, the tape of the meeting also remained as material for the ongoing education of the people of southwest Rockford. It was edited with analysis provided by several members of the community, one of whom concluded the tape by saying,

> The meeting that concluded the project, at least for this year, also renewed it for another year. [The meeting] is a testimonial to the success of the project. . . . We were able to bring together a large number of members of the community, [people] of disparate philosophies, of different organizations, even of different religious persuasions, people who range from both ends of the political spectrum, in terms ranging from stark conservatives to raving radicals; and then we were able to successfully meet with, communicate with, and win out over a bureaucratic system which had already determined, without consultation with us, what they were going to do in terms of the project that was very important to us as a community. I see the interactive media project to be ongoing, not just next year, but years after. What it has introduced to the community is a sophisticated means of approaching one of the most important institutions in our modern culture, which is the electronic media [Niemi and Stephans, 1979, p. 48].

Not all of the battles were won. But even in defeat, we observed a greater willingness among those with whom we worked to engage in the struggle as the battle continues. People with newly found voices are like lions let loose. Video, in the hands of the community, projects these voices. Those who have begun to use it have found an appropriate tool for developing educational materials for empowerment.

Afterthoughts on Technological Solutions

An early concern in planning the Rockford Project was that video would become a necessary tool without which the community again would be reduced to silence. Dependence on relatively expensive and complicated technology would, when the equipment broke down or became unavailable, inevitably lead to further frustration of community goals. The purpose of liberatory education, after all, is not to arm an oppressed population with technological substitutes for their own political literacy, but to develop the personal and collective leadership of the people themselves. In fact, this dependency on video technology did not occur. Small victories achieved through the project strengthened the resolve and confidence of most of the trainees (Wagner,

1974). They became less likely to turn immediately to video as essential to the resolution of community concerns, not only because the bulky and heavy equipment inhibited frequent and spontaneous use, but also because they recognized that it was ultimately their voices that influenced public policy, not the recorder and video monitor.

Video had been used to legitimize action and to validate experience. Many participants in the project had commented that they had not been able really to see their neighborhood and its problems until they saw it on television — a sorry comment on the cultural dominance and power of mass media. But, ironically, video not only legitimized and validated the environment, it also validated the people and their own voices as well. The tapes produced were educational materials in the most liberating sense; that is, they provided a reflective view of the community's struggles as well as the strengths which the community could bring to bear on the task of problem solving.

Clearly, high technology is not the only means (or even the best means) for providing this reflective and self-critical perspective. Audio recordings, photography, and the visual arts — especially drawing and mural painting — provide equally effective materials for liberatory learning and have the added advantage over video of being low-cost, inalienable, and as available as a cassette recorder, camera, or marking pen (Barndt, 1980; Marino, 1979). The decisive factor is not the sophistication of the product (as in conventional media) but the "fresh, intense, nonprofessional, open, committed involvement of people" (Ohliger, 1974, p. 3) in the production of materials for their own learning. Hopefully, continuing educators committed to changing the situation of oppressed groups, and not merely adapting them to situations that leave them marginal, will encourage the development by learners of materials for learning and action.

References

Barndt, D. *Education and Social Change: A Photographic Study of Peru.* Toronto: Kendall/Hunt, 1980.

Freire, P. *Pedagogy of the Oppressed.* New York: Seabury, 1970.

Gwyn, S. *Film, Videotape, and Social Change.* St. Johns, Newfoundland: Memorial University, 1972.

Hopkins, J., Evans, C., Herman, S., and Kirk, J. *Video in Community Development.* London: Ovum, 1972.

Hopkinson, P. *The Role of Film in Development.* Paris: United Nations Education, Science, and Cultural Organization, 1971.

Marino, D. *Drawing from Action for Action: Drawing and Discussion as a Popular Research Tool.* Participatory Research Project Working Paper Six. Toronto: International Council for Adult Education, 1979.

Niemi, J., and Stephans, S. *The Rockford Interactive Media Project.* DeKalb: Northern Illinois University, College of Continuing Education, 1979.

Ohliger, J. "The Media Activists." Paper presented to Unit Administrators Meeting, Educational Communications Division, University of Wisconsin–Madison, February 13, 1974. (Available from Basic Choices, Inc., 1121 University Ave., Madison, WI 53715.)

Theodore, T. "Social and Political Intervention: Video Field Experience." *Mass Media/ Adult Education,* Fall-Winter 1977–1978, *46,* 21–36.

Wagner, R. M. K. *The Social Animator + VTR = Communication??* Saskatoon: University of Saskatchewan, 1974.

Thomas W. Heaney is the director of the community services office of the College of Continuing Education at Northern Illinois University. He has participated in the founding of several community-based adult and continuing education centers and is the president of Basic Choices/Chicago, a center for relating postsecondary resources to the struggles of impoverished neighborhoods in Chicago.

Educators have only superficially tapped computers as a source of
learning materials, yet the computer is inherently a high-level,
personalized learning environment.

Computers and Materials for Teaching Adults Problem Solving

Rex A. Thomas

The winter of 1981–1982 should have been proclaimed the winter of Rubik's Cube. Thousands of puzzle solvers (and nonsolvers) of all ages attacked the little beast. It commanded millions of hours of attention and provided a major source of recreation. Like most other time-consuming pastimes, the educational value of the cube was openly questioned.

The cube seemed to provide an opportunity for learners to inspect their problem-solving processes. Revelations such as "I had to learn to retreat to make a gain" and "I learned how to do parts and, after some practice, was able to put the parts together" indicate that some puzzlers made immediate, if not transferable, growth in problem solving. However, as a laboratory for developing problem-solving skills, the cube did not appear to be very efficient. For many learners, it did not provide sufficient feedback to reinforce desirable general strategies, and the specific skills that were learned appeared to have no practical application.

The educational value of Rubik's Cube has recently been given a new perspective. Golomb (1982) states that the movement of the corners of the cube is a model of the behavior of a hypothetical subatomic particle called a quark. Past students of physics have had to develop an understanding of

J. P. Wilson (Ed.). *Materials for Teaching Adults: Selection, Development, and Use.* New Directions for Continuing Education, no. 17. San Francisco: Jossey-Bass, March 1983.

quarks through vague descriptions and complex mathematical models. Now, assuming the cube has integrity as a model, grade-school children are developing the foundations for understanding not only the quark's behavior but also the vague descriptions and mathematical models as well. Now the initial formal level of learning of these future physicists can increase from the gathering of isolated information to integrating the new knowledge into a familiar model created by playing with a cube.

Golomb's innovative view of the instructional potential of the cube should serve as a model for educators. He found in a common device a vehicle for learning a difficult concept. A promising resource for finding and creating similar models is the computer. Computer-based learning environments can be created that enable the learner to explore within a realistic and bounded domain. They permit each learner to individually structure the materials in a manner that is compatible with his or her needs and previous experiences. In so doing, they free the instructor to serve as an adviser or consultant. The computer offers an opportunity for continuing educators to assume the andragogical approach that leaders have been advocating and teachers have been struggling to understand and implement.

Inherently, the computer is a high-level learning environment. A person learning to program the computer must formulate his or her interpretation of how a computer operates, express that interpretation to the machine, and receive an evaluation. If the interpretation is faulty, it may be due to a lack of understanding of the way the computer functions or merely to a flaw in the form of the communication. The evaluation is a model for teaching behavior because it is direct and immediate about facts and skills and reflective about higher-level aspects. If a learner enters a statement into the computer in an illegal form, the computer simply responds that the statement is in error and indicates the nature of the error. On the other hand, if a learner enters a statement that results in a different outcome than expected, the computer reflects this. It is the responsibility of the learner to alter the model as it pertains to that statement.

The computer is sufficiently versatile to enable educators to develop learning environments that extend far beyond computer operations, yet have the same desirable characteristics. Programs have been written to model phenomena in most academic disciplines as well as many other aspects of society. However, educators have only superficially tapped this source of learning materials and have done very little to develop a learning/instructing model to capitalize on it. The reason for this oversight is probably due to our mistaken view that learning and teaching are inseparable, if not synonymous, and the resulting failure to realize that learning starts before teaching and extends far beyond it.

If Rubik's Cube adequately models the behavior of subatomic particles, a learner who manipulates the cube activates and associates previous learning, identifies areas of deficiencies in that knowledge, and gains insights into how the parts fit together. The principles of physics, when formalized, fit into place like the last piece in a section of a jigsaw puzzle. This activity, which relates previous experiences of the learner (probably in a unique manner), is beyond our capability as instructors; yet, it seems an essential prerequisite to the learning process. It prepares the learner in advance and does not require a postinstruction struggle to fit the pieces together. In some cases, at least, computer-based models can fill that gap.

A second gap that is rarely filled by traditional instruction is the integration of acquired knowledge into a usable form. A multitude of professional seminars possess this characteristic. In far too many instances a learner is left with fragmented ideas, skills in need of practice, and concepts that are not fully understood. Only when a learner returns to the job does he or she have an opportunity to apply and integrate the newly learned material. Unfortunately, the maxim that "experience is the best teacher" needs many qualifications. Few formal instructional experiences can be coordinated with the work environment closely enough in nature and time to permit adequate integration. Computer models can provide needed experience and can provide it, in many respects, in an instructionally optimum manner.

Activities for Developing Problem-Solving Skills

To illustrate the use of a computer-based learning environment, activities for developing problem-solving skills will be explored. The general process to be promoted incorporates the following steps suggested by Polya (1957):

- Understanding the problem; identifying the known, unknown, and conditions
- Devising a plan drawn from previous experiences or a restatement of the problem
- Carrying out the plan
- Looking back to verify the accuracy of the result, discover an overlooked shortcut, and generalize or expand the method.

Although these steps were devised for teaching problem solving in mathematics, they are applicable to a wide range of problems. Nearly all adult learners can improve their problem-solving skills by recognizing and identifying shortcomings, reviewing the basic procedure, and adopting the practice of reflecting on successes and failures.

To clarify the role of the learner, computer, and instructor, the game Brain Teaser, developed and marketed by Edutek Corporation, will be used. This implementation is not ideally suited to the learning of problem-solving methods (Thomas, in press); however, the game itself has some excellent features. It requires the learning of a set of primitives and the building of higher-level tools. If offers distractors that magnify the learner's shortcomings. It also models learning situations found in important subject areas such as mathematics and physics.

The Brain Teaser puzzle consists of a three by three array of squares that may either be orange or black. The array is displayed on the computer screen. The squares may be changed from one color to the other by moving the cursor with the game paddle to a desired square and pressing the paddle button. The object of the game is to create a pattern of an orange square in the middle and black squares around the outside. The pattern of squares is shown in Figure 1.

If the cursor is placed in a corner square (1, 3, 7, 9) it changes the color of that square and the three squares adjacent to it. For example, placing the cursor in square 1 would change the color of 1, 2, 4, and 5. If the cursor is placed in an outside square that is not a corner (2, 4, 6, 8) it changes the color of all squares along that side. Placing the cursor in square 5 changes the color of squares 2, 4, 5, 6, and 8. The cursor can only be placed in a black square, so if all of the squares are orange, the game is over.

Although Brain Teaser seems simple, it is really quite challenging for most learners. The common practice is to race through the introduction of the basic operations and then make a series of random moves with the hope of achieving success. The motion is hypnotizing, and random moves are easy to conceive; thus, many students do not progress beyond this stage. The successful learner, however, practices the basic moves until their outcomes are predictable, then turns off the computer and devises a plan.

The only state that can precede the final state is shown in Figure 2, where the cursor can be placed in the center square to solve the puzzle. Once a learner realizes this, a series of states in a success tree can be identified. On returning to the computer, the learner can look for known states that lead to success. Thus, random activity is replaced by insightful and purposeful activity. With persistence, a learner can establish a sequence of moves that lead from any solvable state to the solution. (In a matrix of this type, there are 512

Figure 1. Brain Teaser Display

1	2	3
4	5	6
7	8	9

possible states; however, due to symmetry, only 128 are unique and one of those is unsolvable.)

When Brain Teaser has been used by the author as a predecessor to formal instruction on problem solving, it has revealed to the learner a need for improving problem-solving skills. It has illustrated the importance of understanding the givens and the goal. It has vividly illuminated a need for advance planning and for patience in executing the plan. With Polya's (1957) first three steps having been experienced, a discussion of the successes and failures demonstrates the value of looking back.

For the instructor, this exercise provides an opportunity as well as a challenge. It opens the door to formalize and verbalize the steps and pitfalls in problem solving for an interested and receptive clientele. It reveals the strengths and weaknesses of each individual to both the instructor and the learner.

Effective use of the computer in this manner creates a role for the instructor that is quite different from a lecturer or a subject matter authority. Implicit is the assumption that falling into a shallow padded hole is much more effective for learning than listening to the description of a deep and dangerous cavern. It requires an operating philosophy far beyond and, in many respects, diametrically opposed to the behaviorist philosophy on which most instruction is based. Rubinstein (1980, p. 37) sheds light on this role in advising that "some questions are so outstanding that they should not be spoiled by a direct answer." The instruction must uncover the deficiency or the discovery that stimulated the question and encourage both the process by which the student arrived at that point and the action that will maximize generalization. This requires that instructors have confidence in their own problem-solving skills as well as confidence in the learner.

In addition to serving as a preinstruction activity, Brain Teaser can serve as an integrating exercise that follows formal instruction. Learners

Figure 2. State that Precedes Solution

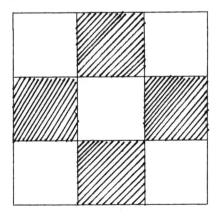

familiar with the steps in problem solving can apply those steps to the Brain Teaser puzzle. In this case as well, the instructor's role is to help the student learn to develop and refine the problem-solving process, not to help the student memorize the steps.

Computer-based materials designed specifically to support experientiation and integration are not abundant. Due to the nature of computer programs, and because experientiation and integration closely parallel vocational activities, materials that can be adapted may be more common than one would assume. Programs designed as vocational tools, such as business or forecasting models, require the user to supply values such as interest rates, cost of labor, cost of raw materials, and projected sales, and computes the estimated profit or loss. A neophyte manipulating the model can gain valuable insight into the relationship and relative effects of the variables. A more experienced learner can test hypotheses and evaluate his or her command of the subject.

Computer programs for modeling or projecting are available in many areas, including agriculture, finance, economics, and business. Some are too complex for introductory instruction, whereas others are well within the reach of creative educators. Use of these programs will serve to define the instructional role and to stimulate the design and development of more appropriate computer-based learning environments.

The instructional value of the Rubik's Cube and Brain Teaser are probably serendipitous. Nevertheless, they open the door of opportunity. They reveal a level of individualized learning that is far beyond traditional instructional capability. They move the focus of instruction from the teacher to the learner. The cube identifies an important aspect of learning that is commonly overlooked, and Brain Teaser demonstrates the computer's potential as a learning aid. In so doing, these games present a challenge to our stale and inadequate, although comfortable, methods of teaching.

The willingness of continuing educators to meet the challenge to study the computer and to use it to enhance the learning process will influence whether this generation of educators takes a step forward toward a respectable profession or a step backward toward a poorly paid skill.

References

Golomb, S. W. "Rubik's Cube and Quarks." *American Scientist,* 1982, *70,* 257–259.
Polya, G. *How to Solve It.* New York: Doubleday, 1957.
Rubinstein, M. F. "A Decade of Experience in Teaching an Interdisciplinary Problem-Solving Course." In D. T. Duna and R. Reif (Eds.), *Problem Solving and Education: Issues in Teaching and Research.* Hillsdale, N.J.: Lawrence Erlbaum Associates, 1980.
Thomas, R. A. "Review of Brain Teaser. " *The Journal of Courseware Review,* in press.

Rex A. Thomas received his Ph.D. from Iowa State University, taught high school mathematics, and has been a computer programmer in industry. He is currently professor in professional studies and a member of the Computation Center staff at Iowa State University.

If we are indeed on the threshold of becoming a learning society,
the preparation and selection of materials that will encourage
successful learning through the lifespan is of unusual importance.

Materials for Nontraditional Study and the Natural Learning of Adults

Charles A. Wedemeyer

The emergence of a learning society (National Research Council, 1978; Wedemeyer, 1981) places increasing emphasis on the materials used for learning by adults. Learning is a natural, continually developing, renewable behavior throughout the lifespan. Learning tends to be idiosyncratic in style and process for each learner, although the basic stages are thought to be consistent.

Learning and Schooling

Traditional schooling attempts to encourage learning for all by grouping learners largely by age. However, mass schooling for all requires the admission of all, regardless of ability; hence, schools tend to have very heterogeneous populations of learners. Consequently, schools should introduce some degree of individualized instruction to accommodate all learners.

When learning is carried out in nontraditional ways (that is, outside the confines and environment of the school and classroom, with teacher and learner separated in space and time), the same dilemma exists. For example, correspondence study is a method that is intended to reach learners at a distance from the teaching institution. Generally, a learner's age, situation, place

J. P. Wilson (Ed.). *Materials for Teaching Adults: Selection, Development, and Use.* New Directions
for Continuing Education, no. 17. San Francisco: Jossey-Bass, March 1983.

of residence, and previous experience are relatively immaterial, depending upon the purposes of a given course. This openness of opportunity implies that any learner can be accommodated and can be provided with instruction and materials that will bring about learning.

But, as noted earlier, learning tends to be highly personalized and idiosyncratic to individuals. Recognizing this, another authority (Holmberg, 1981, p. 30) perceives correspondence study as a process of "guided didactic conversation," carried on at a distance. Earlier, Wedemeyer (1962, p. 15) noted that "correspondence study, at its best, is personal tutoring carried on by mail."

Whether the materials provided to the distance learner are mass-produced units, guided didactic conversations, or personal tutoring, their effectiveness depends on linking them to an instructional system that is capable of individualization. The selection of appropriate technology can provide more than accelerated communication. Interactive computer-assisted instruction can make possible an acceptable degree of individualization (Scanlon and others, 1982), but so can the didactic notes, letters, and telephone calls of a teacher working with carefully prepared and selected materials for distance learners. Mass materials development and selection requires special effort and understanding.

The burgeoning adult learning phenomenon — from fully independent learners conducting their own self-initiated projects (Tough, 1971; Gross, 1977; Wedemeyer, 1981) to learners enrolled in traditional and nontraditional learning programs offered by a wide variety of institutions — underscores the importance of appropriate learning materials. Adult nontraditional learners are different from learners in school. Adult nontraditional learners need learning materials prepared and selected according to their maturity, concerns, situational characteristics, motivations, previous experiences, roles, and behaviors. Wedemeyer (1981) contrasted thirteen differences of traditional and nontraditional learners in a way that has implications for the preparation and selection of materials.

In nearly a century of correspondence study, the problem of preparing and selecting appropriate materials has resulted in specialized procedures. Research has been initiated to analyze the characteristics of successful materials preparation, selection, and evaluation. Holmberg's (1981) bibliographies on course development, structure, style, and typography provide useful sources of research into these topics throughout the world, for these are worldwide problems. His related discussions of these topics define the problems and the state of the art in finding solutions.

The Role of Specialists

The preparation and selection of materials in formal courses are usually guided by experienced specialists. Modern course materials preparation involves many areas such as subject matter, instructional design, media and communication graphics, materials composition and design, and production. Materials may be prepared in various media—print, audio, visual, computer programs—or in articulated multimedia combinations. Even when audio and visual media are employed, print is usually basic to all materials preparation and selection.

The necessary contributions of so many specialists in the preparation of materials leads to conflicts: Whose criteria are to prevail in case of disagreement? How can conflicting viewpoints be accommodated? It used to be assumed that the subject matter specialist would prevail because the teacher and subject matter were central, but now concern for learning and the needs of the learner have moved into a more equal position. The course team concept employed by Britain's Open University has garnered much support throughout the world because of the high quality and effectiveness of the materials produced by this process.

But even course teams have their problems. Subject matter, learning, communication, instruction, learner situations and characteristics, goal-setting, evaluation, media, production, and priorities are not inherently simple. Melding together such a broad range of complex matters for teamwork and decisionmaking is difficult and demanding. A candid and penetrating report (Oates, 1982) on Open University course development concerns and activities contains sections on a course team chairman's viewpoint: why students don't learn, learning from audiovisual media, computer-assisted learning, student learning difficulties and support services, student learning, diversity and the institution, and adult learning and continuing education. While the Oates report's focus is not specifically on materials, the report clearly demonstrates the interconnectedness of all course team activities and the interrelatedness of everything that goes into the development and production of course materials.

Other Patterns

Most providers of learning materials for adults do not work from a course team format. Smaller organizations may place almost total responsibility in the hands of a single specialist-manager, leaving to that person the responsibility for all phases of development and selection. Institutions with strong academic traditions still tend to place most responsibility for all phases of development and selection on the subject matter specialist guided by a coordinator. But nearly every provider has found it necessary to seek assistance in the development of at least a manual of guidelines for the preparation or selection of materials—a clear indication of the importance and difficulty of materials development.

Formative evaluation has been suggested (Wedemeyer, 1981) for guiding and monitoring the development of learning materials that express the institution's goals and concern for quality yet are shaped to meet the needs, goals, roles, and behaviors of learners. As more is learned about these aspects of adult learners, the trend toward more complex processes in the development of learning materials will continue and accelerate.

Adult learners who plan and carry out their own learning find their materials wherever they can. These do-it-yourselfers are in the grand tradition of self-made (meaning self-educated) Americans. In a country in which nearly everyone is an immigrant or the descendent of immigrants "the American Dream meant the opportunity to become what one could become... that meant self-initiated learning, self-development, preparation for that better time that lay ahead" (Wedemeyer, 1981, p. 218). For thousands of adult learners it is still that way. What kinds of learning materials succeed with self-directing learners?

Guidelines for Materials Development

Guidelines for practitioners emerge from the literature on course materials development and also from such related fields as communications and linguistics. The guidelines that follow are representative of current wisdom in the field. Of course, there are conflicting views and practices and research studies are sometimes contradictory. There is no unanimity among practitioners and specialists on many matters.

Purpose and Goals. Materials are developed to directly involve the learner in the activities of a course or project. Materials may also be used to individualize instruction in a course by involving the learner in the choice of materials according to personal interests, level of ability and goals, and the choice of activities derived from the materials. It is well known that a significant impediment to learning is the number of learners who fail to understand or correctly employ course materials. Even when the objectives of educational materials are carefully supplied, many learners do not achieve because they cannot understand the academic writing in which objectives are presented.

Intelligible Materials, Comprehending Learners. There are two fulcrums for levering learning from materials: developing intelligible materials that can be understood by large groups of learners, and improving the reading, listening, and viewing skills of learners so that they can comprehend more difficult materials.

Readability. Readibility is the study of materials to measure and predict their intelligibility to the learner. With roots going back to Thorndike, readability become popular after World War II, when the educational system was growing rapidly. In 1953 the cloze readability procedure was developed (Taylor, 1953); a more adequate method of measuring the difficulty of passages. Holmes (1982) described the use of the cloze procedure in a readability project in New Zealand. The following recommendations emerged:

1. Use words familiar to students.
2. Avoid unnecessary clauses beginning with *which* or *that*.
3. Shorten long sentences (they confuse students).
4. Use only one complex idea in a sentence.
5. Do not use words of three or more syllables unless necessary.
6. Avoid the passive tense.
7. Relate the material to the student.
8. Avoid using many prepositions and adverbs; avoid jargon.
9. Use active verbs.

Linguistics. Linguistic science, as a field of inquiry into human language, meaning, and comprehension, has also made contributions to the development and selection of materials for learning. The following guidelines for materials development and selection are based on sound linguistic principles.

1. Intelligibility is improved by simple sentence structure, simple grammar, simple vocabulary, and short clauses.

2. Material should be organized for coherence and logical flow.

3. Material is more effective when it takes the learner from known to unknown in short, clear steps.

4. The repetition of new concepts, ideas, or information will speed comprehension and remembering. However, too much repetition (called redundancy) leads to a slowing of comprehension. The materials developer should use redundancy carefully, but avoid long-windedness.

5. Succinctness and relevance to the learner's characteristics, interests, concerns, and goals adds stimulation and motivates the learner to persist.

6. Learner comprehension is an active, constructive, and even creative process. The learner's activity consists of a number of cognitive subprocesses initiated from an information base, added to by elaboration, modified by reduction, internalized by processing, and reinforced and evaluated by retrieval and application.

7. The learner's background knowledge, general ability level, and motivational and study competence are significant in processing knowledge. What the learner brings to the study of materials is as important to progress in learning as the materials are. If the materials are prepared for the level of competence that the learner already has, the materials will work better than if pitched too high or too low.

8. With the recommendations of Holmes's (1982) guidelines, academic writing can be tailored to suit the capabilities of the majority of learners.

9. Linguistic studies confirm that clause relationships are frequently misunderstood, and are a common cause of poor comprehension.

10. Expository text should be broken up into strategic units followed by review questions. Questions appearing *after* the relevant material stimulate more careful reading, slower learning, and contribute to a more general learn-

ing effect. However, questions that merely check facts tend to encourage rote and surface learning. Questions should encourage the learner to think independently, formulate new ideas, and develop solutions to problems. In some way not yet understood, questions and the places they are inserted affect the intelligibility of text.

11. Attention-getting graphic devices used in texts and margins seem to have some merit in signaling the learner about the status and relative importance of the communication. Such signals may operate to some extent as questions do in helping the reader to plan, modify, and execute reading strategies. They may also be useful aids in controlled redundancy. Key words in the margin to denote essential concepts, italics, underlining, or caps are also facilitating signals and redundancies. However, other studies suggest that attention-getter graphics and "supersigns" have disadvantages — they may distract learners, cause them to concentrate on reading related to the signal, and reduce thinking and depth learning.

12. Learners grasp positive statements more easily than negative. Declarative sentences are preferred over interrogative. Abstract nouns should be avoided. Adjectives slow comprehension, but pronouns speed it.

13. Density or compactness of text (the number of words per unit of information) should be moderate.

14. Text and pictures (or other graphics), articulated together, are useful in increasing comprehension. Such texts have also been found to be useful with audio instructions; each strengthening the other.

Troubling Questions Remain

This brief summary of guidelines for developing materials requires further comment. There are two approaches for the improvement of learning from the use of materials: The materials can be made more effective, and the learning skills of those who learn from materials can be made more effective. While empirical studies confirm the usefulness of adapting materials to the ability and characteristic needs of the learner, there is also some uneasiness about the long-term effects of this process. One needs only to look at mass radio, television, film, and publishing to glimpse the problem. In our zeal to concentrate on making materials fit the learner's condition and needs, are we to some extent designing materials around learning handicaps rather than learning strengths? And if materials are designed to be effective at the level of handicap, will growth in ability be regressive rather than progressive over time?

Materials skillfully matched with language, vocabulary, grammar, reading, writing and other deficiencies in targeted learners do succeed, empirically, at deficiency levels. But, will the long-term use of materials so designed keep learners at deficiency levels?

The other approach—improving learner reading, writing, listening, viewing, and thinking skills—is obviously just as important in accelerating learning through the use of materials. Libraries, for example, are filled with materials that are useful and important, but beyond the ability of the people who need them. Do we work to improve reading skills so that more people are brought within range of needed materials, or do we adapt the materials downward in skill and ability requirements so that deficient readers can read them? The continuing slide in learner achievement in basic skills means that deficient learners will have to try to improve themselves through self-study later on as adults. The danger is that the most readable texts and materials—those skillfully adapted to the level of learner ability (which may, in fact, be a level of deficiency)—may stifle thinking, growth, and development. The perfect material at any level is in one sense a complete system of learning. It doesn't require anything from learners except what is already there, and so may fix the learner in a position of arrested development, dependence, and deficiency. In fashioning materials, can we be so enamored of professional, other-directed learning that we overlook the power and persistence of natural, self-directed learning?

There are good positions on both sides of this baffling problem. As the needs of a learning society confront us, the developers of learning materials will have to make important decisions that will greatly affect the material for learning through the lifespan.

References

Gross, R. *The Lifelong Learner.* New York: Simon and Schuster, 1977.

Holmberg, B. *Status and Trends of Distance Education.* London: Kogan Page, 1981.

Holmes, N. "The Readability of Study Materials: Recent Research in New Zealand." In J. S. Daniel, M. A. Strand, and J. R. Thompson (Eds.), *Learning at a Distance, A World Perspective.* Edmonton, Alberta: Athabasca University-ICDE, 1982.

National Research Council. *Telecommunications for Metropolitan Areas: Opportunities for the 1980s.* Washington, D.C.: National Academy of Science, 1978.

Oates, J. (Ed.). *Student Learning from Different Media in the Open University.* Teaching at a Distance Institutional Research Review, No. 1. Milton Keynes, England: The Open University, 1982.

Scanlon, E., Jones, A., O'Shea, T., Murphy, P., Whitelegg, L., and Vincent, T. "Computer Assisted Learning." In J. Oates (Ed.), *Student Learning from Different Media in the Open University.* Teaching at a Distance Institutional Research Review, No. 1. Milton Keynes, England: The Open University, 1982.

Taylor, W. L. "Cloze Procedure: A New Tool for Measuring Readability." *Journalism Quarterly,* 1953, *30,* 415–433.

Tough, A. *The Adult's Learning Projects: A Fresh Approach to Theory and Practice in Adult Learning.* Toronto: Ontario Institute for Studies in Education, 1971.

Wedemeyer, C. A. "Learning by Mail." *Writer's Digest,* 1962, *42* (9).

Wedemeyer, C. A. *Learning at the Back Door: Reflections on Non-Traditional Learning in the Lifespan.* Madison: University of Wisconsin Press, 1981.

Charles A. Wedemeyer is the William H. Lighty professor of education, emeritus, at the University of Wisconsin, Madison, and Extension. As a teacher, administrator, and scholar, he has spent much of his career working on adult, nontraditional learning and the development of innovative learning systems. He was a pioneer in independent, open, and distance education institutions. His most recent book is Learning at the Back Door: Reflections on Non-Traditional Learning in the Lifespan.

Self-directed learning is almost universal. Characteristics
of self-directed learning have to be considered in developing
educational materials that can meet the needs of adult learners.

Educational Materials
Development and Use with
Self-Directed Learners

Susan T. Rydell

Creating educational materials for use with self-directed learners is both challenging and paradoxical. It is challenging because self-directed learning is so pervasive, with an infinite potential of topics; and it is paradoxical because in materials design it is the author who determines materials content, format, and organization. Yet, self-directed learning implies that the learner makes these determinations as well as others.

This chapter will provide an overview of prominent research findings related to self-directed learning. A discussion of materials for teaching self-directedness and use with self-directed learners will follow.

Research on Self-Directed Learning

Research on self-directed learning is relatively recent. While the importance of studying self-directed learning has been affirmed (Tough, 1971), little is known about how adult learners actually use the various identified resources in their learning projects, the problems they confront in their learning, what kind of assistance is needed, and how learners evaluate their learning (Cross, 1981). Smith (1982) concludes: "Research in self-directed learning

J. P. Wilson (Ed.). *Materials for Teaching Adults: Selection, Development, and Use.* New Directions
for Continuing Education, no. 17. San Francisco: Jossey-Bass, March 1983.

projects is rudimentary in design and limited in the sophistication of the questions which have been asked. . . . The research is largely cumulative on the one hand (with no larger organizing context) and probing on the other hand (still looking for the right questions)" (pp. 45–46).

Although our knowledge about self-directed learning and the study of it is limited, research has produced some relatively consistent findings (Cross, 1981). It is reported that from 79 percent (Penland, 1977) to 100 percent (Coolican, 1974, 1975) of all adults conduct at least one learning project each year. Typically, adults conduct five projects per year and spend about 100 hours on each. About 74 percent of learning projects are completely self-directed, 15 percent involve group learning, 10 percent are in one-to-one situations, and 3 percent utilize preprogrammed, nonhuman resources such as tapes, programmed instruction, or television. Only 20 percent of all learning projects are planned by a professional who is paid or institutionally designated to facilitate the learning (Tough, 1978). The research does help to spell out some general characteristics of self-directed learning.

Characteristics of Self-Directed Learning

Self-directed learning is generally viewed as intentional learning in which the person's major goal is to "gain and retain certain fairly clear knowledge and skill, or to produce some other lasting change in himself" (Tough, 1971, p. 6). Self-directed learning is initiated by the learner, and it is the learner who determines what is to be learned and how that learning will be achieved. When adults plan their own learning activities, they do so to respond to their own perceived learning needs: to solve an immediate problem rather than learn a formal academic subject. Most self-directed learning is in practical areas such as improving reading, clerical, mechanical, or vocational skills, or developing avocational interests such as gardening or crafts. Other self-directed learning relates to topics of close personal interest such as family, interpersonal relations, psychology, and religion. While a number of people may be consulted at various phases of the learning endeavor, courses or other group learning activities may also be a part of the learning plan. Adult self-directed learners will view themselves, not their teachers, as the primary "drivers" of the activity (Knowles, 1975).

The contexts in which self-directed learning occurs are very broad. Many self-directed learners are found in noncredit community education courses, taking classes ranging from cake decorating to how to operate a home computer. They are also found in college programs designed specifically to meet the needs of returning adult students. In addition, programs in continuing professional education are making efforts to provide the flexibility demanded by adult learners. Many self-directed learners, however, will not be enrolled in any readily identifiable learning activity, and they may be using resources found through their jobs, libraries, or other community resources.

Individual adult learners will pick and choose from the range of potential learning resources those which best fit their immediate learning needs. Preexisting educational materials may not be available for any given learning project. Research on the use of educational materials for self-directed learning may never parallel that in the relatively controlled environment of the teaching machine/programmed text/computer-assisted instruction tradition. However, counselors, teachers, librarians, and others in positions requiring knowledge of adult learners and their learning needs can provide insights into the types of materials requested and used. Materials developers at agencies and institutions will find discussions with such resource persons invaluable in developing materials for a particular clientele within a given organizational context.

Materials to Teach Self-Directedness

Many current educational materials for adult learners have been devised under the basic assumption that self-directed learning is something that can be taught. These materials tend to focus on process-oriented variables such as goal-setting and developing self-assessment skills, rather than on discipline-oriented content such as data processing, mathematics, or English.

Many devices exist in a community that tend to assist people in developing self-directed learning skills for use within a particular context. Examples include map/locators found in subways, shopping centers, and college campuses. Other examples include materials used in orientation programs in libraries and museums. While devices and materials used in these situations may teach people some skills about how to acquire new information in similar situations, that is not their original intent.

Other materials are designed for the purposes of teaching learners knowledge and skills that will have applicability beyond the immediate teaching-learning situation. Generally, these materials include components of developing personal goal setting and learning how-to-learn-skills. This type of material includes support materials for career-life planning programs and extension or programs for adults returning to college. One example is ENCORE, the Council for the Advancement of Experiential Learning's (CAEL) computer-assisted system for adults with work or life experiences who want to explore career and educational options and find out how to gather evidence of prior learning. ENCORE was designed by JoAnn Harris-Bowlsbey and links with DISCOVER II and SIGI, which provide detailed information on careers.

While ENCORE was created to be used in a variety of provider agencies for direct or referral services, many academic institutions develop study guides that assist returning adult students in developing goal-setting and self-assessment skills. The content of these guides is presented within the framework of the institutions' specific academic policies, procedures, and educational philosophy. Most frequently, the guides are used as support materials in an orientation program, portfolio development course, or educational planning courses. The Union for Experimenting Colleges and Universities' *Learners Handbook,* Marylhurst College for Lifelong Learning's *Portfolio Development Guide,* Ohio University's *A Study Guide for Portfolio Development—Independent Study,* and Metropolitan State University's *Individualized Educational Planning* textbook are examples of such materials. Other institutions, such as Moorhead State University in Minnesota, use packets and handouts in their educational planning course.

Materials for Self-Directed Learners

Most materials on today's educational materials market have been designed and packaged to present specific subject matter. The content generally reflects the interests of the author/instructor and the delivery mode, such as an independent study course or a computer-assisted or computer-managed instruction module (such as PLATO), may be responsive to the flexibility and self-pacing needs of adult learners. However, individualized instruction and self-paced delivery should not be confused with self-directed learning. Self-directed learners may determine that all or a portion of a prepackaged course meets their learning needs. On the other hand, self-directed learners may choose a number of alternative learning strategies.

Increasingly, libraries have become an important source of materials for self-directed learners. Historically, libraries have served the major information needs of academic institutions, corporations, businesses, the government and special service agencies, and the general public. The role of libraries has moved away from being merely repositories for books, documents, and nonprint materials, toward becoming centers providing general and specialized information services. The information center role of libraries has been enhanced by technological advances allowing access to a variety of computerized data bases.

Several major public library systems, including the Denver Public Library and the Tulsa City-County Library, have initiated library-assisted self-directed learning programs. In these programs, individual learners meet with a librarian to discuss personal learning needs and receive help in using the library and locating community resources. New York state libraries have been involved with a number of projects, including complementing employment skills provided by CETA, providing services for adults interested in career change, and providing information and referral for independent learners ("Libraries and Adult Learners," 1982).

Materials Development for Self-Directed Learners

A number of variables should be considered when developing educational materials for use by self-directed learners.

Purpose. As is the case for all instructional materials development, the purpose must be clear. Also, in addition to the usual design considerations, variables of interest to the developer and the potential adult learner-user become factors. For example, some provider agencies are reaching out to adult clienteles as the numbers of their traditional eighteen- to twenty-two-year-old students decline. Materials developed for such purposes may have a primary aim of attracting new students and/or reducing instructional costs by decreasing the time span of faculty involvement. Adult students tend to want to learn at their own pace and to have some flexibility in the selection of time and place of the learning. Such factors should be considered very early. Matters related to institutional and organizational policy can be agreed to prior to the actual materials planning.

Assumptions about Self-Directed Learning. In the early phases of educational materials development, attention should be given to the assumptions one is willing to make about the nature of self-directed learning. To what extent is it assumed that adult students know very little about how to be self-directed learners and that the goal is to assist them in acquiring this skill? To what extent is it assumed that because students are adults they have a fairly high level of self-directedness, and that the task is to harness this ability? Perhaps one of these questions relates to the mission and goals of your organization or to your institution's educational philosophy.

Tensions with content experts or faculty subject specialists need to be resolved in discussions of assumptions about self-directed learning. When educational materials are used in credit-bearing courses, the final authority of faculty members over course content may seem at odds with academic rhetoric about opportunities for self-directed learning.

Know the Learners. What do you know about the learning needs and learning styles of your clientele? Frequently, this information can be based on observation and informal discussions with potential materials users. Some continuing education participants will travel great distances to use materials, while others want materials that can be used at home. Most adult students want materials that will, in some way, save them time, either in the actual time it takes to use the materials or in the overall time to acquire the desired knowledge or skills. These considerations will influence the packaging and delivery of the materials.

Knowing the backgrounds of potential students in areas for which materials are being developed will help identify the content of what is prepared. Some adult students feel as though they have certain skills (such as counseling), but that they lack a broad-based theoretical knowledge. They seek educational materials that provide a conceptual framework and deemphasize the development of practical skills. In other cases, as in the area of political science, students may have had theoretical courses but now seek practical skills related to an applied area such as working on a political campaign.

Transfer of Learning. In all work with self-directed learners, it is important to consider the degree to which the learner is expected to generalize beyond the immediate teaching-learning environment. This is particularly true in the development of educational materials because materials will influence the instructional design. As noted earlier, adult students, particularly those engaged in self-directed learning projects, tend to have pragmatic concerns and initiate learning activities to solve immediate problems. While educators may aspire to instilling lifelong learning skills in their students, the students themselves may view the content knowledge as an end in itself. Providing completely prepackaged, self-paced courses may reinforce a student's dependence on institutions and educational materials. On the other hand, materials that give students latitude in subtopics to be selected or options to find resources on their own will assist them in becoming more confident self-directed learners.

Conclusions and Implications

Characteristics of self-directed learning, results of research on self-directed learning, and the assumptions we are willing to make about self-directedness all have implications for educational materials.

The following summary observations may assist the continuing educator in finalizing the format and content of materials being developed.

1. Review your responses to the issues raised earlier in this article. These are issues to be reviewed very seriously at a project's inception; they should not be backed into at a materials testing phase.

2. Examine the potential costs. If you consider truly self-directed learning as that in which learners define the problem, identify resources, and acquire the desired knowledge and skills, then preparing educational materials — in the hope that they will be used at some time by someone — becomes an extremely costly endeavor. Taking advantage of existing resources and referring students to them can substantially reduce costs. With appropriate direction, students can use complementary films, audio cassettes, computer programs, and print materials within your provider agency or in external agencies. Metropolitan State University recently completed courses coordinated with the Minneapolis Public Library's three-year National Endowment for the Humanities (NEH) funded learning library program, "Minneapolis: Portrait of a Lifestyle." The only materials costs to the university were for detailed handouts for students on the library's program and related readings. The library program provided the films, videotapes, bibliographies, community workshops and tours, keynote speakers, and so on. The courses taught by university faculty members paralleled and supplemented the community-based resources and materials (Meyers and Raedeke, 1981), and within several courses, students completed self-directed learning projects meeting their own individualized learning goals.

3. Build in flexibility. Given the competing demands on adult students' time and differences in student learning styles and learning goals,

flexibility is essential. Continuing educators frequently find that designing materials in modules gives students flexibility in completing the work and instructors flexibility in revising the material. Opportunities for access to learning by students with diverse backgrounds and interests are likely to be expanded. Modules, in turn, may refer students to external resources or to other prepackaged materials, thus providing students flexibility in content. Flexibility in material content and delivery should also include the option of giving students structure and deadlines, if that is what is most effective for the learners in a particular context.

Developing educational materials for use with self-directed learners presents exciting opportunities for continuing educators. As more is learned about how learners use identified resources and the specific kinds of assistance they need in completing their learning projects, we will be able to refine the material produced so that it can best meet the needs of self-directing learners.

References

Coolican, P. M. *Self-Planned Learning: Implications for the Future of Adult Education.* Syracuse, N.Y.: Educational Policy Research Center, Syracuse University Research Corporation, 1974.

Coolican, P. M. *Self-Planned Learning: Implications for the Future of Adult Education* (Addendum to the 1974 paper.) Washington, D.C.: Division of Adult Education, U.S. Office of Education, 1975.

Cross, K. P. *Adults as Learners.* San Francisco: Jossey-Bass, 1981.

Knowles, M. S. *Self-Directed Learning.* Chicago: Follett, 1975.

"Libraries and Adult Learners." *The Bookmark,* 1982, *40* (3), entire volume.

Meyers, M., and Raedeke, A. "A Public Library and a University Team Up to Offer a Unique Program." *Library Resource Sharing,* Occasional Papers of the Minnesota Library Association, no. 2, 1981.

Penland, P. *Individual Self-Planned Learning in America.* Washington, D.C.: Office of Education, U.S. Department of Health, Education, and Welfare, 1977.

Smith, P. "A Literature Review of Self-Directed Learning Projects." Unpublished qualifying paper, Harvard University, Graduate School of Education, 1982.

Tough, A. *The Adult's Learning Projects: A Fresh Approach to Theory and Practice in Adult Learning.* Research in Education Series, no. 1. Toronto: Ontario Institute for Studies in Education, 1971.

Tough, A. "Major Learning Efforts: Recent Research and Future Directions." In *The Adult Learner: Current Issues in Higher Education* (selected papers from the 1978 American Association for Higher Education national conference). Washington, D.C.: American Association for Higher Education, 1978.

Susan T. Rydell is a psychologist and professor in the Individualized B.A. Program at Metropolitan State University in St. Paul, Minnesota. She was a charter faculty member of Metropolitan State and has served in several administrative positions, most recently as associate dean for learning resources. At the University of Minnesota, she developed multimedia materials for teacher training for use by local, state, and national organizations.

The point of self-assessment is to have a clearer sense of purpose
and a renewed commitment to live an effective and satisfying life.

Self-Assessment in Educational Programs for Adults

Leo Goldman

Because adults enroll in educational programs for many different reasons and purposes, it follows that the self-assessment activities used in these programs can run the entire gamut from standardized tests to informal games and exercises. There are, in fact, almost a limitless number and variety of methods to help individuals to assess their abilities, interests, values, goals, and life-styles. The word *limitless* is literally accurately here, because so many of the assessment methods that are useful for adults have been developed by teachers, counselors, and other practitioners for their own use, and only a very small percentage have been published. The continuing educator, therefore, can expect to find assessment methods in books, journals, newsletters, and also can learn of them by attending workshops and conferences and acquiring catalogues from the many publishers of educational materials.

The emphasis in this chapter will be on these informal methods rather than on standardized tests. The main reason is that most adults participating in continuing education programs find these informal assessment experiences far more valuable than standardized tests, which have, for the most part, been developed for use with children and adolescents. Adults are usually less concerned with (and get less out of) the paper-and-pencil measurement of various mental abilities than with the exploration of interests, values, alternative life-styles, methods of handling stress, and ways of satisfying personal and social

J. P. Wilson (Ed.). *Materials for Teaching Adults: Selection, Development, and Use.* New Directions for Continuing Education, no. 17. San Francisco: Jossey-Bass, March 1983.

needs. Another important reason for the emphasis here is that the informal methods can be used to some extent by almost all educators, whereas standardized tests properly should be used by or under the supervision of a specialist in assessment—usually a counselor or psychologist.

Finally, the informal methods usually involve the individual much more actively in the process of assessment than do standardized tests; this is highly desirable at all ages, but especially so with adults who typically come with some sense of purpose and goal and therefore are more ready to participate actively in sharpening their purposes and goals and in finding ways to realize them.

The self-assessment methods described here may be used in various ways—as an activity in almost any continuing education course; in courses specifically designed for self-exploration, career planning, and other personal development purposes; or in one-to-one or small counseling group settings. Also the methods included here focus on the positive—seeking strength and growth—rather than diagnosing pathology or seeking negative factors in the individual's life history.

Career Planning and Changing

Increasingly, adults feel the need or find it necessary to review their career status several times during their working lives. Many indeed seek educational experiences that will help prepare them for a different career—whether because job opportunities in their field have decreased, or their occupation has changed in ways that make it no longer attractive or feasible for them to continue, or simply because they feel ready for a change.

Whatever the case, there are several types of assessment devices and methods that are useful. However, one type that is not dealt with here is the entire area of abilities. For the most part, adults can assess their abilities by reviewing past experiences on the job and in school. Occasionally, tests of general mental ability or specific aptitudes are indicated; if so, it is probably wise that they be administered as part of a professional vocational counseling service.

Interest Exploration. There are a number of standardized interest inventories in use. (See the Buros *Mental Measurement Yearbooks* for a complete list.) Most are intended to compare the individual's responses to a number of like-dislike questions with those of a sample of people in general or with samples of people in specific occupations. Two will be singled out for mention here as probably being most useful for adults and for self-assessment.

The *Strong-Campbell Interest Inventory* (Campbell and Hanson, 1981) stands almost alone in its research base and frequent updating. The individual receives a profile showing the degree of similarity of his or her interests to those of people in a number of different occupations. Most of the scoring services also offer a printout that interprets the scores verbally much as a counselor would do, though a professional counselor would go on to explore implications with the individual. The main value of the SCII is that it does provide comparison with adults actually participating in various occupations.

A very different kind of inventory is exemplified by the *Hall Occupational Orientation Inventory* (Hall and Tarrier, 1976). More so than most published inventories, this one is intended to encourage and facilitiate exploration by each individual, preferably in a group where the members can compare values, interests, and experiences and learn from each other. The manual offers many suggestions for individual exploration, and the inventory is being recommended for this aspect rather than for its measurement or normative qualities.

Counselors and others have developed many exercises and games to help individuals become aware of their interests. One in particular that has been more elaborately developed than most and that is of outstanding value is the *Vocational Card Sort*. One version is the Non-Sexist Vocational Card Sort (Dewey, 1974). Although standardized procedures and a set of materials are suggested, these may be modified by the user at will because there is no quantitative scoring to be concerned with. The individual sorts a number of cards containing occupational titles (seventy-six in the Dewey system) first into "would consider," "would not consider," and "uncertain" piles; then subsorts the "would consider" and "would not consider" files into clusters, each of which contains cards that have in common the reasons for choosing or rejecting them. The richness of this method lies in the individual's complete freedom to project onto the occupations whatever work values, goals, and interests reside in that individual's makeup and perceptions. The optimal application of this method requires the leadership of a skilled counselor, since this is as much a counseling as an assessment technique. Groups are an ideal setting for the VCS, and the flexibility of the method makes it adaptable for any age group.

Workbooks. There are many workbooks commercially published, and many others produced locally, that lead the individual through an assessment process. Certainly the most thoroughly researched of these is *The Self-Directed Search* (SDS) (Holland, 1977). The individual is led through brief self-ratings of abilities and interests and arrives at a profile that then may be compared with profiles considered appropriate for various occupations. In effect, this method simulates, in abbreviated form and with subjective judgments rather than formal measures, the process that a counselor might go through with a client.

Quite a different type of workbook is exemplified by the College Board's *Deciding* (Gellatt and others, 1972). Where the SDS attempts to quantify the self-assessment process and bypass the counselor, *Deciding* is intended mostly to be used in groups under the leadership of a counselor or other group leader. Included in *Deciding* are activities and discussion related to values exploration, decision-making processes, methods of obtaining career information, choosing a job, and other topics. Many workbooks of this type have been written or assembled at schools, colleges, and other institutions for their own use.

Career Maturity Inventories. Although designed mainly for use with adolescents, career maturity or career development inventories can be useful with adults who have not yet completed such developmental tasks as being acquainted with the general structure of the world of work, knowing the sequence of stages one goes through in preparing for and entering an occupation, knowing how to use various resources in obtaining information and making choices, and knowing how to assess one's career-related characteristics. Among the major inventories at present are the *Career Maturity Inventory* (Crites, 1978) and the *Career Development Inventory* (Thompson and others, 1981). Used with vocationally immature adults, these inventories may help to identify the individual's stage of development regarding career and to spotlight the specific kinds of assessment and learning activities needed by that person.

Computer Programs. Probably the most elaborate and thoroughgoing self-assessment materials are those available via computer. One very well-developed program is System of Interactive Guidance and Information (SIGI) (Katz, 1981). This is a complex program that is set up for each college and is built around that college's characteristics, but some of the basic processes are similar to other computer programs for career planning. The person, seated at the computer terminal and facing a screen, might first choose to explore work values (such as security, high income, interesting work) in a dynamic process by assigning weights to each value, then having an opportunity to examine the resulting profile and reassign weights. The person might next request information about occupations related to his or her profile of values. Following that (or skipping it if desired), the individual might call up detailed information about programs at that particular college, including specific statements of probability as to the grades that person is likely to obtain in each program, based on data about the individual's test scores and previous grades that are already entered into the computer data base.

Personal Explorations

Many adults are interested in exploring one or more facets of their lives other than the career area. These facets might include values, lifestyle, use of time, handling of stress, relationships with family and friends, leisure activities, planning for the next steps in their lives, and others. There seems to be a never-ending flow of pamphlets, films, and other materials in this area. All we can do here is select a few examples that include assessment of the individual's status with reference to aspects of living such as those mentioned above.

Although there are some commercially published materials in this area, for the most part the activities seem to be homemade or acquired at workshops. (In this connection the author would like to acknowledge as a source of some of these materials the Sagamore Institute, 110 Spring Street, Saratoga Springs, New York 12866, which conducts workshops and publishes a good deal of material in this area.)

In the values area, an interesting activity is the "values auction," which can be adapted for different groups and settings. Essentially it is conducted much in the way an auction of tangible items would be, but what is auctioned are such intangibles as a lifetime of security, peace for the world, political power, an ideal personal relationship, many friendships, and so on. Each participant may spend a designated amount of money in any way he or she chooses and may even be given play money to make it seem more realistic. Immediately afterward, a debriefing session is held, during which the participants are asked to examine their feelings and thoughts about the various values and also their feelings about the competitive experience of the auction itself.

There are many other approaches to helping people examine their values. An activity that exemplifies one approach is the "kidney machine game," of which there are many variations. Participants receive thumbnail sketches of perhaps eight or ten individuals each of whom requires the use of a kidney machine (dialyzer) in order to survive but only one of whom can have access to it. Working in small groups, the participants must decide, in effect, which person shall live. The candidates for the machine exemplify various values: important public service, rare professional skill, youth, being the parent of young children, artistic talent, and so on. The debriefing following the group's decision encourages the participants to study the implications not only of the values with which each individual identified, but also of the way each person functioned in the group discussion. This latter point bears emphasis: Almost every exercise, game, or other activity used for assessment of whatever is the content of that activity also offers an opportunity to look at the way the person functioned, related to others, and felt during the activity. That assessment information may be as important as assessment in relation to the content.

Some assessment approaches are a kind of self-inventory. One example in the area of assessing friendship patterns is a simple but potentially powerful inventory that consists of a list of names of one's closest friends. For each friend, one indicates such information as the person's sex, age, ethnic background, occupation, religion, how long known, how often seen, last time seen, marital status, who initiated the friendship and who tends to maintain it, and what kinds of activities one engages in with each of the friends. After completing the list, the individual studies it for trends and patterns that can be very revealing. Then the group can be organized into pairs or triads, each person telling one or more things that were a surprise or stating one change that person would like to make in friendship patterns—perhaps to broaden the network of friends, become more of an initiator, and so on. As a next step the total group might meet together and individuals volunteer to discuss some of those same things.

An activity that helps people to assess their patterns of handling stress includes asking them to write answers to the following questions: What words do you associate to the word *stress*? What causes stress in you? What are the effects of stress on your mind, body and behavior? How do you relax when feeling stress? The teacher, or whoever else is the leader of the group, might ask for volunteers to give answers to some of these questions before going on to the next one, or the participants might be asked to work in twos or threes to exchange answers to specific questions.

This is but a tiny sample of the great number and diversity of activities for helping adults to assess their personal and social characteristics. Some of the books listed at the end of this chapter (Figler, 1979; Simon, Howe, and Kirschenbaum, 1978; Stanford, 1977) contain many such activities, but even those are merely a fraction of those that have been developed and used. The interested continuing educator can continue to expand the repertoire by attending selected workshops and conferences and scanning publishers' catalogues for books on this subject.

Follow-Through

The assumption throughout this chapter is that self-assessment of adults is merely a means to an end. The end is greater self-knowledge, and perhaps a specific decision or enrichment in one's daily life. The materials and activities that were selected for description here are the ones that seem most likely to promote these ends. Standardized tests rarely accomplish that, in large measure because they are convergent in nature and tend to close off thinking on a subject rather than open it up. Some may protest that the subjective methods are less precise and lack evidence of validity. In fact, both the precision and the validity of most standardized tests are so limited that there is no great loss.

The follow-through is therefore important. It requires a tone that is positive and that anticipates growth rather than dwelling on problems or on assigning blame for one's sad state of affairs. Setting and maintaining such a tone mainly is the responsibility of the leader. The group itself can be a great source of support as each individual begins to make plans for change and commitments to action. For some, these changes will include taking courses; for others, changing careers or starting a business; and for still others, changing their personal lives in some ways. That, after all, is the point of self-assessment — to have a clearer sense of purpose and a renewed commitment to live a more effective and satisfying life.

References

Buros, O. K. (Ed.). *Mental Measurement Yearbooks.* Lincoln: University of Nebraska, 1953, 1959, 1965, 1972, 1978.

Campbell, D. P., and Hanson, J. C. *Manual for SVID-SCII.* (3rd ed.) Stanford, Calif.: Stanford University Press, 1981.

Crites, J. O. *Career Maturity Inventory.* Monterey, Calif.: CTB/McGraw Hill, 1978.

Dewey, C. R. "Non-Sexist Vocational Card Sort." *Personnel Guidance Journal,* 1974, *52,* 311–315.

Figler, H. *Path: A Career Workbook for Liberal Arts Students.* Cranston, R.I.: Carroll, 1979.

Gellatt, H. B., Varenhorst, B., and Carey, R. *Deciding.* New York: College Entrance Examination Board, 1972.

Hall, L. G., and Tarrier, R. B. *Counselor's Manual: Hall Occupational Orientation Inventory.* Bensenville, Ill.: Scholastic Testing Service, 1976.

Holland, J. *The Self-Directed Search.* Palo Alto, Calif.: Consulting Psychologists Press, 1977.

Katz, M. R. *System of Interactive Guidance and Information.* (4th ed.) Princeton, N.J.: Educational Testing Service, 1981.

Simon, S., Howe, L., and Kirschenbaum, H. *Values Clarification: A Handbook of Practical Strategies for Teachers and Students.* (2nd ed.) New York: A & W Publishers, 1978.

Stanford, G. *Developing Effective Classroom Groups: A Practical Guide for Teachers.* New York: A & W Publishers, 1977.

Thompson, A. S., Super, D. E., Lindeman, R. H., Jordaan, J. P., and Myers, R. A. *Career Development Inventory.* Palo Alto, Calif.: Consulting Psychologist Press, 1981.

Leo Goldman, now professor in the graduate school of education of Fordham University, was until recently a professor in the graduate school of the City University of New York, where his duties included directing the program of continuing professional education. He is the author of Using Tests in Counseling *and a number of articles in counseling journals about tests and measurements. He has held office in several organizations, including the Association for Measurement and Evaluation in Guidance and the American Psychological Association, and was editor of* Personnel and Guidance Journal.

Aging is accompanied by changes in receiving, processing, and responding to information and thus requires special considerations for effective materials use.

Adapting Materials Use to Physical and Psychological Changes in Older Learners

Don C. Charles

Teaching older adults can be a rewarding experience for an instructor, especially one who has usually taught younger learners. But does the instructor need to have any special proficiencies in presentation or organization of classroom materials because the learners are in their fifties or beyond? In general, is there anything really special about older learners? The answer (as is so often the case in education) is not clearly "yes" or "no," but a little of both. "Yes," because there are some negative changes in sensory and motor functions and in cognitive processing that have implications for dealing with the physical and intellectual environment. "No," because older learners are more like than unlike younger learners, and because what is good for older learners is usually also good (if not so necessary) for young ones.

Psychologists, and especially those concerned with the years past youth (gerontologists), have explored these changes extensively and there is much published research. While direct implications of some of the work are not readily apparent, much can be inferred that is of practical use in the classroom. The person functions as a unified whole, but it is practical to consider some attributes and systems separately, in line with available research emphases. Here we will examine changes in the capacity to receive information,

J. P. Wilson (Ed.). *Materials for Teaching Adults: Selection, Development, and Use.* New Directions for Continuing Education, no. 17. San Francisco: Jossey-Bass, March 1983.

to process information, and to respond appropriately and efficiently. In addition, we will consider some noncognitive factors that influence classroom performance. In each of the functioning areas, suggestions will be made for improving the efficiency of use of various kinds of classroom materials for the older learner.

Receiving Information

"I can see as well as ever, but my arms are getting too short." "My hearing is all right, but everybody seems to mumble these days." The frequency of comments of this kind suggests something of the extent of our awareness of common age changes. Obviously, one needs little scholarly evidence to recognize that sensory functions become less efficient with age. But what losses are functionally important, and which ones are trivial nuisances? What kinds of compensation are helpful in responding to these universal changes? While all the senses have been explored to some extent, we will focus here on vision and hearing, the obvious concerns in the classroom.

We will describe the usual changes occurring in the normal, healthy, late-middle-aged adult. The longer one lives, the more chance that trauma will occur in any functional domain, but space does not permit discussion here of a variety of common disorders related to sense perception, such as cataracts, diabetes, or stroke. Each such condition poses special problems and requires special responses.

Vision. The entire structure of the eye changes steadily throughout life, with reduced visual efficiency during late and middle and older age. In addition, the perceptual processing mechanisms of the brain also decline, particularly in the speed with which they process incoming information. We will consider some of the consequences of these changes.

General Acuity. Precision or clarity of vision declines through most of adult life, and after seventy, "poor vision is the rule rather than the exception" (Botwinick, 1978, p. 143). Thus, printed or projected material must be composed of figures or letters that are easily read, spaced adequately so they do not interfere with each other, and are as uncluttered and straightforward as is consistent with their content.

Presbyopia. Loss of elasticity of the lens leads to the farsightedness common to nearly all aging persons. Actually, the process has been going on since childhood, but it is usually in the late forties or fifties that we are forced to recognize and deal with the change and get our first bifocals or reading glasses. This takes care of the problem in a way, since distance vision is not affected and the bifocals take care of near vision. But not all stimuli are near enough or far enough to fit. For example, many professional associations have "poster sessions" at their conventions; areas in which researchers are allowed a few square feet of board on which to display summaries of their work. Large figures present no problems, but some presenters simply post typed summaries of their work. Aging observers (including this author) find themselves skipping those displays or attempting to elevate the head to a painful angle to try to aim the bifocals at the material. It should be apparent to the instructor that eye-level material to be examined at arm's length or so will not be perceived readily if the print or figures are small enough to require bifocal magnification.

Light Sensitivity. Simply put, the older person needs a much higher level of illumination than does a young one. This is true both for general room lighting and for the material to be focused on. Also, glare from a shiny surface may efface details more completely for older people than for young ones (McFarland, 1968).

Depth Perception. Stereopsis, the ability to detect differences in the placement of objects, declines fairly rapidly after forty or fifty. This is not usually a problem in the classroom, where materials are often displayed on screens or boards, but might cause difficulty with models, mockups, simulations, and so on, where physical space perception becomes a factor (Fozard and others, 1977).

Dark Adaptation. The rate at which one adjusts to darkness following light not only slows significantly with age (during the second minute of darkness, young subjects are five times as sensitive as old), but the ultimate level of adaptation is poorer. Thus the classroom or laboratory should have some constant level of illumination even though it needs to be partially darkened for film showing or other activities, and learners should not be forced to find their way through a darkened room or corridor (McFarland, 1968).

Color Vision. The principal problem here is increasing confusion in the blue-green range. Older learners should be not expected to make subtle distinctions of color of this sort (Botwinick, 1978).

Hearing. Human hearing in our society begins to decline in the late teens, especially in males, and this decline is continuous throughout life. Specific structural or functional problems may attack individuals, but we all share a loss of neural transmission to the perceptual areas of the brain and increasingly less efficient processing of what is transmitted. That deterioration is selective and results in what is called *Presbycusis*—a loss in ability to hear higher sound frequencies. A normal young adult will hear from 20 to 20,000 Hz (or cycles per second). Losses will be relatively insignificant below 1,000 Hz (about two octaves above middle C) by age fifty, but will increase after that. For higher frequencies, the loss is much greater and increases faster: At age sixty, it is difficult to hear a tone an octave higher than the highest on the piano keyboard (8,000 Hz) (Botwinick, 1978). Since the sound range of the human voice is generally lower than these, we might assume that while we lose the ability to hear the higher pitches of the violin, we still hear speech adequately. Unfortunately, this is not the case.

The ability to understand speech remains relatively constant between ages twenty and fifty, but after that, decline is steady so that by eighty, understanding has been reduced by 25 percent (Feldman and Reger, 1967). Consonants are especially difficult to discriminate (McFarland, 1968).

Speech Perception. There is a difference between the ability to hear pure tones on the laboratory audiometer and the ability to comprehend the complex sounds around us. Rees and Botwinick (1971) found that young and old adults did not differ in their ability to detect pure tones masked with other sound, but older adults were less effective in reaching decision criteria, presumably because of processing changes or cautiousness.

Surroundings. Due to the above circumstances, the aural surroundings of the older learner become even more important than for a younger counterpart. The "cocktail party phenomenon," a babble of voices, laughter, and the comings and goings of numerous people leaves us trying to look interested and intelligent as we look at an animated face talking at us, while the meaning of the words is lost in the general confusion of sounds. This is the experience the older person may have from less confused sounds heard at a lower volume level. Any kind of background noise will interfere with understanding, such as hissing radiators or rattling fans, passing traffic, or whispering in the room.

Minimizing Problems. From research of the kind cited above and from experience with older learners, a number of suggestions can be made to improve communication. First, the place of instruction must be as quiet as possible; when this is not practical, as in a field experience, the learners will need additional, perhaps one-to-one instruction to make up what they missed. The volume of presentation must be high enough to suit the room but not so high as to create too much reverberation. Because of slower and less efficient processing, the rate of speech must be deliberately slowed. (In talking to seriously deaf persons, it is far more important to slow our rate of speech than to talk louder.) Where prerecorded material (films or tapes) is used, repetition may be necessary since the rate of speech cannot be slowed. Because older people are often unwilling to admit they do not understand, it is vital to probe to determine that they really are registering the material adequately.

Processing Information

"Processing" means utilizing or disposing of information or stimulation that has been received; the brain must develop a concept, solve a problem, put into memory, or in some fashion process the continuous flow of information received. This is an area of complex and often esoteric study, but one simple, straightforward, and important generalization can be made: With increasing age, more time is required for the processing to occur. Thus, the instructor of older learners must always remember to keep the rate of presentation and the response requirement at a level that is comfortable for the students. But there are a number of other adjustments that may be made, many having to do with the nature of the stimulus or material presented.

Simplicity or Complexity. As the material presented—whether auditory or visual—becomes more complex, all learners have more difficulty and take more time to deal with it. However, the increase in difficulty and time is much greater for old than young learners (Botwinick, 1978). Therefore, it is desirable to simplify content as much as possible. This is not to remove the meaning from inherently difficult ideas or problems, but to present parts sequentially, focus on one aspect at a time, or in some other fashion reduce the load being presented at one time. For example, a complicated diagram with many reciprocal interactions pictured might be broken down into several coherent diagrams and then assembled in the final and complex form. The instructor will have to find out by asking questions and probing what constitutes an overload for a particular group of learners—chronological age is not by itself sufficient information. Education, prior experience, and fatigue all have their effect. (Anyone who has taught adults for several hours in an evening class after a day's work recognizes the need for lightening the load as the hours pass.)

Nature of the Task. Other modifications of the task may be made in response to processing changes. One of these is to reduce abstraction. Arenberg (1968) found that framing the task and the required solution in concrete rather than abstract form helped elderly learners more than younger ones. The use of diagrams, models, representations, and the like are obviously part of this process.

Another research finding is that the introduction of irrelevant information into instruction or task organization causes confusion and inefficiency; older people do not discriminate as well as young. Asides, interpolations, or peripheral and nonessential material sometimes added thoughtlessly or with the notion of breaking monotony must be examined carefully to be sure they do not serve to confuse, rather than amuse or relax the students. Such material may be useful overall in maintaining a pleasant atmosphere, but it is important to separate it clearly from the task at hand.

A related matter is eliminating redundant material—needlessly repetitive or overly-illustrated—because it may cause confusion in the learner (Rabbitt, 1965).

Another matter of importance is pacing; as noted above, the presentation must be slower for elderly learners than for young. Numerous studies reveal that self-pacing is ideal, and produces better results than other controlled speeds. This is where the computer comes into its own as a method of instructing older adults, of course, but in the traditional classroom the teacher can only be particularly sensitive to whether the group as a whole is lagging, impatient, or on target as figures, slides, or other materials are presented.

Responding

Response is considered in the same light as processing, since the same term (slowing) and the same cause (processing) is the major consideration. Slowing is independent both of sensory modality and the type of responses required (Botwinick, 1978). The villian of the piece is not primarily the muscles or peripheral nerve net, but inevitable change in the central nervous system.

The speed and efficiency with which stimuli are interpreted, decisions made, and responses instituted become progressively slower with age (Birren and others, 1980).

Because it is the decision-making process that is a major cause of slowing, well-learned and familiar tasks show little change with age. The older automobile driver, for example, will shift gears in response to engine labor about as efficiently and quickly as he did decades earlier. The same man, however, may be a far less efficient learner and a slower performer at the computer console than will his teenaged son.

How do we respond to this situation in continuing education, other than by allotting more time for older learners? One part of the response is to discuss the problem with learners, assuring them that their slowness, especially with motor responses, is not evidence that they cannot learn but rather evidence that they need to take a somewhat different, and more leisurely, approach to the task. Then the instructor should provide drills or repetition sufficient to bring them to proficiency on the task at hand, such as by practicing on a model computer keyboard until the location of symbol and function keys does not require long consideration or decisionmaking.

In other words, whatever can be done to reduce the newness of any required response (by individual practice or by modifying the response) will increase the speed and quality of the learner's response. Materials that can be placed in the hands of the learners, such as worksheets, role guides, or even sequentially organized transparencies can be of great assistance here.

Noncognitive Factors

As we know from our own experience, intellectual capacity is only one of many factors involved in performing learning tasks. Under the general heading of noncognitive factors, a number of research studies have evaluated the influence of some of these factors. Okun (1980) reviews these under the topics of cohort-associated factors, motivation, and task characteristics.

Cohort-Related Factors. A cohort is simply a group of persons born about the same time, for our purpose, more than fifty years ago. The factors that are highly cohort-related include health and vigor, occupation, and general personality traits. All of these should be considered when designing teaching materials. For example, from the author's off-campus teaching experience, a class composed of nursing instructors or trainers might respond well to projected tables, figures, and relatively complex data presentations, while a class composed of housewives newly returning to the educational experience might not be comfortable with much more than generally instructive films.

Motivation. The data are somewhat conflicting here, in that some older learners display insufficient arousal and some show too much. Obviously, the first condition prevents real involvement and the latter leads to confusion and inefficiency. Cautiousness is a widespread trait among older learners; they are very likely to err on the side of nonresponse for fear of responding incorrectly. Thus every effort should be made to solicit responses from these learners and to exercise care that responding will be positively rewarded even if errors are made. Tests are likely to be stressful for older learners and arouse considerable anxiety. Thus, they need a warm and supportive atmosphere, one in which tests are used as learning devices rather than as purely judgmental experiences.

Task Variables. It is particularly important that instructions are clearly understood. Because of problems discussed earlier, some lack of understanding may occur. Older learners are less likely to report their lack of understanding and, indeed, may report that they understand when they do not. Thus it is desirable to elicit "for instances" from them or to have them try a simplified example of the task to be sure they understand.

Some Recommended Reading

There is a rapidly-growing body of psychological research on all aspects of aging, but much of it is not scientifically sound nor does it have application for the classroom. A good source that has positive recommendations based on research is a chapter entitled "Aids and Types of Learning" (Botwinick, 1978, pp. 282–310). A review of several aspects of learning in maturity is presented in a symposium, "Educational Psychology and the Adult Learner," edited by Charles (1980). The *International Journal of Educational Gerontology* is, as its title suggests, devoted entirely to this topic, and its current and past volumes are a rich source of observations and research on learning in older persons.

References

Arenberg, D. "Concept Problem Solving in Young and Old Adults." *Journal of Gerontology,* 1968, *23,* 279–282.
Birren, J., Woods, A. M., and Williams, M. V. "Behavioral Slowing with Age: Causes, Organization, and Consequences." In L. Poon (Ed.), *Aging in the 1980s.* Washington, D.C.: American Psychological Association, 1980.
Botwinick, J. *Aging and Behavior.* (2nd ed.). New York: Springer, 1978.
Charles, D. "Educational Psychology and the Adult Learner." *Contemporary Educational Psychology,* 1980, *5* (4), 289–404.
Feldman, R. M., and Reger, S. N. "Relations Among Hearing, Reaction Time, and Age." *Journal of Speech and Hearing Research,* 1967, *10,* 479–495.
Fozard, J. L., Wolf, E., Bell, B., McFarland, R., and Podolsky, S. "Visual Perception and Communication." In J. Birren and K. W. Schaie (Eds.), *Handbook of the Psychology of Aging.* New York: Van Nostrand Reinhold, 1977.
McFarland, R. A. "The Sensory and Perceptual Processes in Aging." In K. W. Schaie (Ed.), *Theory and Methods of Research on Aging.* Morgantown: West Virginia University, 1968.

Okun, M. A. "The Role of Non-Cognitive Factors in the Cognitive Performance of Older Adults." *Contemporary Educational Psychology,* 1980, *5,* 321–345.

Rabbitt, P. "An Age Decrement in the Ability to Ignore Irrelevant Information." *Journal of Gerontology,* 1965, *20,* 223–238.

Rees, J. N., and Botwinick, J. "Detection and Decision Factors in Auditory Behavior of the Elderly." *Journal of Gerontology,* 1971, *26,* 133–136.

Don C. Charles is professor of psychology and education,
Iowa State University, Ames Iowa; a fellow of the American
Psychological Association division on developmental psychology,
educational psychology, and adult development and aging,
and a fellow of the Gerontological Society of America.

*"He who imagines all fruits ripen at the same time
as the strawberries, knows nothing about grapes"
(Paracelsus, 1493—1541).*

Selection and Use of Materials in Adult Basic Education Literacy Instruction

Florence W. Carmen

Adult students differ in academic ability, age, sex, background, goals, interests, and motivation. Selecting teaching strategies and materials for topics that adults want to learn is challenging.

Jerome Bruner (Hechinger, 1981, p. 65) describes the educator's task as "the mining of human potential." He asks: How can we teach in a way that does justice to the diversity of students? How can we keep interests alive and provide skills that contribute to students' needs and to society? How can we know the real interests and goals of students?

Teachers and Materials

A large-scale evaluation of four reading systems developed for functionally illiterate adults was done in 1965. This cooperative research project, involving the Office of Economic Opportunity, the Welfare Administration, the Office of Education, and Greenleigh Associates was conducted in Califor-

Permission was granted by the author's students, whose writing is included in this chapter. Students' names are withheld by request.

J. P. Wilson (Ed.). *Materials for Teaching Adults: Selection, Development, and Use.* New Directions for Continuing Education, no. 17. San Francisco: Jossey-Bass, March 1983.

nia, New Jersey, and New York. State education departments, local school districts, and over thirty governmental jurisdictions were involved. Over 1,100 students were assigned and completed the seventeen weeks of classroom instruction.

Highlights of Findings

1. "There were no significant differences in student gain scores by reading systems" (Greenleigh Associates, Inc., 1966, p. 15). No particular reading system contributed more than another to a positive educational and social experience for the learner.

2. "A high school graduate can be as effective as a certified elementary school teacher in teaching adults to read" (p. 18).

3. "On the basis of observation, it seems that teachers of adult basic education should be selected for their warmth, interest, motivation, flexibility, understanding, and patience" (p. 17). "A combination of teacher enthusiasm, group solidarity, and good supportive services rather than the reading system itself provided a high level of interest" (p. 17).

It is interesting that features of the instructor and the social environment can play such a significant role in the effectiveness of various instructional materials. It seems important, therefore, that, before focusing on materials for teaching reading in adult basic education (ABE), we first examine learner–teacher relationships.

Learner–Teacher Relationships

In 1982 Malcolm Knowles described his method of facilitating self-directed learning. Unless students agree to be more responsible for their own learning, learning cannot take place at all. The teacher must develop a set of skills that require "relationship building, needs assessment, learner involvement in planning, linking of students to learning resources, and encouraging learner initiative" (Knowles, p. 2).

Techniques developed by Paolo Freire, the radical Brazilian educator, encouraged people to unite to talk about their problems (Freire, 1970). He devoted his life to the advancement of the fortunes of the impoverished people of Brazil and Chile. His theory for educating illiterate adults was that people are capable of looking critically at their world. In this way, they will change the structure of society that oppresses them. The correct method lies in dialogue. "The teacher is no longer merely the-one-who-teaches but one who is himself taught in dialogue with the students" (Freire, 1970, p. 67). "Students — no longer docile listeners — are now critical coinvestigators in dialogue with the teacher" (p. 68). He went further: He encouraged the transformation of the world. Teaching was a means of helping victims of oppression to change their situation in an unjust society.

George S. Counts (Dennis and Eaton, 1980) also sees the educator as social critic and reformer. His primary concern is with social change. Teachers and teacher unions would be the means of constructing this new society; methodology should be secondary. The emphasis should be on ideas and understanding; education never should be separated from the broad social process of change in the community.

Men and women should be encouraged to be agents of their own education and learning. Developing an atmosphere of mutual respect and trust between students, as well as between the students and the teacher, is necessary for success in adult basic education. There is more to teaching than the selection of printed material.

Instruction should be challenging and motivating, at a level where students can succeed. Failure is acutely painful; therefore, adult participants should experience some success each time they attend class. The teacher should stress achievement, not failure; recognize effort, determination, and regular progress in some tangible way.

Far more could be said about the relationships among learners and between learners and teachers and about how these relationships are established. Discussion — simply talking about interests and problems — is probably the most effective way of building trust and rapport. Without these conditions, the effectiveness of teaching and learning is reduced, as is the effectiveness of even proved materials.

Having discussed the instructional setting, we can now focus more closely on educational materials. What should we look for in educational materials for use in teaching in ABE?

Choosing and Evaluating Materials

Whether students have second- or tenth-grade–level reading skills, they invariably have one primary goal: to pass the high school equivalency test. Familiarity with developmental and skill-building programs is important. Testing, conducted as nonthreateningly as possible, is also important. Remember, both boredom and frustration are major causes of students dropping out.

New and innovative instructional programs have been developed and produce results. Today there are materials emphasizing such basic adult educational areas as survival skills, consumer math, and functional English.

It is not difficult to find material; the problem lies with the selection process. Evaluating material, when there is so much to choose from, is a challenge, indeed. All adult basic education material should:

- Be especially developed for adults
- Teach facts and concepts useful to adults and be of high interest
- Develop the learner's self-concept
- State the purpose of the material and the skills it is designed to teach
- State the readability level

- Be clear, precise, legible, grammatically correct, and appropriately illustrated
- Have answers with easy access, so that students can check their own progress
- Have a pretest and a posttest, when appropriate
- Have a process of individualization that allows students to progress at their own speed
- Have a sequence of skills
- Be self-instructional
- Have a good table of contents, index, or both
- Encourage a student to be independent, a self-starter, a self-prescriber, and a self-corrector.

Although many good materials have been selected for high school students, it is important to select materials that students have not failed in.

With regard to teaching reading, materials today are developed especially for adults, even for those at the lowest level. It is no longer necessary to embarrass adults learning basic reading skills by using pictures and content meant for children. You may be teaching new readers, but you are not teaching new learners. Everyone learns to read better by reading. Students should be encouraged to read what interests them.

Life-Centered Education

"Although consumerism has boomed during the last decade, very little consumer education has reached the poor, those who need it the most" (National Association for Public Continuing and Adult Education, 1980, 1982). A study begun in 1971 at the University of Texas at Austin, sponsored by the U.S. Office of Education and completed in 1975, took on the task of defining adult functional literacy and its extent. The result of the cross-national survey yielded a definition of functional competency as the ability to use skills and knowledge needed for meeting the requirements of adult living. Four primary skills are contained in this definition: Communication (reading, writing, speaking-listening, viewing), computation, problem solving, and interpersonal relations.

In an official release related to this study, the Office of Education proclaimed that one out of five American adults lacks the skills and knowledge to function effectively in the basic day-to-day struggle to make a living and to maintain a home and family.

Major adult basic education publishers have developed materials, referred to as the Adult Performance Level (APL) study, based on this joint effort.

New Avenues in Education

Computers are not for every teacher or every student. The teacher must be enthusiastic and actively engaged in organizing material. The use of computers with basic-skills students can be successful, since the computer can act as a patient and tireless drillmaster. An additional advantage is that the student is not publicly embarrassed when errors are revealed.

Computers are on the way to becoming a good teaching–learning tool, but it is necessary to have special instruction in their use. Another drawback is that computer programs are not interchangeable from one manufacturer to another. Manufacturers are scrambling to get computers into the classroom, forming partnerships with educational publishers to develop programs for schools. Both colleges and manufacturers are starting to offer classroom teachers training in the use of computers.

Creative Writing

Reading, writing, spelling, and English can be taught through creative writing. Mistakes made by students are an important source of information about how they use language and how they feel about the world they live in.

People have learned that it is risky to talk or write much about what they think, feel, or worry about. Many adults today, students in prestigious colleges as well as educated adults in all fields, cannot write because they have never had the practice. The New York State Regents Competency Test, a requirement for high school graduation in New York State, now requires students to write three separate exercises.

We learn to write by writing. One of the most important reasons for teaching writing is that it is an opportunity for you as a teacher to share your life with your students, and for your students to share their lives with you. Relationships between students in a group also change and develop in a meaningful way as a result of this sharing.

People who keep journals or write personal letters know that writing is a valuable means of self-discovery. Such writing has a way of requiring one to be honest. People become surer of what they know and do not know, conscious of what they truly believe, and confident of what they want to do.

Teachers should do the same kind of writing they ask their students to do. The students see them struggling to get it down just right, and learn that writing is not magic, it is hard work. One has to think in order to write, to go deep into the depths of oneself. This is an opportunity to put emphasis on feelings and imagination. Language is not describing facts, it is creating images.

What my adult learners write is personal, often beautiful, poetic, sometimes sad or even shocking, and written in simple language. I am always moved as I gain a better understanding of life as it is for them, and feel humble when I read what they are willing to share with me.

In conclusion, and to illustrate this point, some of my ABE participants have given me permission to share some of their writings.

Right from the first grade no teacher ever started
me where I was. I never could keep up with the class.

90

You Hear
I'm to be a person
Not animal.
I'm to be of feelings
Not disrespected.
I'm to be Myself
Not nigger
I'm to be treated by you
As you treat yourself
And in return
I'll do the same.

Outside These Walls
Outside these walls, there's laughter, children play and run;
Inside these walls, there's sadness, you seldom see the sun.
Outside these walls, there's freedom, freedom night and day;
Inside these walls, there's sorrow, suffering in every way.
Outside these walls, there's streets and flowers, trees and cars;
Inside these walls, there's cement, cement and steel bars
Outside these walls, are people, joyous and refined.
Inside these walls, are men, spending life confined.

I think the afternoon when I go home is the best time in the day for me. That's when I get to enjoy my grandchildren. That's when they come out to play in the yard. They get the sun and bring their wagon out, pull it around the house and the sidewalk. I am careful that they don't run in the road. They come over to me, climb up on my lap and take my hand and give me a kiss. That's the best!

Last Summer I went down to South Carolina. It was so hot my little cousin got sunburn and he thought he had some kind of disease. He said to his mother, "Look, Ma, I have some kind of disease." And I said, "Let me see, Randy." I told him, "You don't have any disease, you been sunburn."

Finishing school is like walking through brick walls. I try and try! But my head just will not function the way I would like it to. Now that I'm going to the ABC Center I hope to get my GED—if not I will never get it. I have to try.

Annotated Bibliography for Teachers

Barasovska, J. *I Wish I Could Write*. Syracuse, N.Y.: New Readers Press, 1978.
Ideas for inspiring new writers by a teacher who believed they could write.

Fadiman, C., and Howard, J. *Empty Pages: A Search for Writing Competency in School and Society.* Belmont, Calif.: Fearon Pittman Publishers, 1979.

Literacy Volunteers of America, Inc. *Bibliography of Adult and Teenage Reading Materials, ESL and the Humanities.* Syracuse, N.Y.: Literacy Volunteers of America, 1980.

Basic reading books are arranged according to Adult Performance Level categories and to grade levels. A major addition to the bibliography is the inclusion of books in the field of the humanities selected for new readers. The index includes an alphabetical listing of titles, as well as a directory of publishers.

Weinstein, C., and August, B. *Applied Writing.* New York: Technical College, Division of Continuing Education, City University of New York, 1982.

A writing skills curriculum for adult learners.

Annotated Bibliography for Students

1. Globe Book Co., Inc., 50 West 23rd St., New York, NY 10010.
   a. *World of Vocabulary,* Book A, B, L, 2, 3, 4. Reading level: 2–7.
   b. *A Need to Read: Finding the Main Idea,* Levels A, B, C.
   c. *A Need to Read: Building Vocabulary,* Levels A, B, C.
   d. *A Need to Read: Identifying Details and Sequences,* Levels A, B, C.
      Reading level: 4–9. Have large print and realistic illustrations. Sound, sequential program in reading comprehension.
   e. "Improving Math Competence"
   f. "Reaching Math Comptence"
      A two-book series of step-by-step instruction in performing basic math operations. Solve problems of life related to managing money, shopping, jobs, health, and safety. Large print, well illustrated. Good examples and explanations.
2. Institute for Life Skills Employability Skills Series, Teachers College, Columbia University, Box 138, 525 W. 120th St., New York, NY 10027.
   A system to help develop job-related skills. Aids each participant in attaining knowledge and skills for the successful management of his or her employment search. Includes group discussion, viewing, and critiquing a videotape of her or his own performance in using acquired skills.
3. Jamestown Publishers, P.O. Box 6743, Providence, RI 02940.
   a. *Adult Learner Series: Selections from the Black.*
      Provocative selections by Black writers. Reading level: 6–8.
4. McGraw-Hill Book Co., 1221 Avenue of the Americas, New York, NY 10020.
   a. *Learning 100,* Educational Developmental Laboratories, Inc.
      Use of audiovisual techniques to give the adult student maximum enrichment in a minimum time.
      Instruction in communication skills is the foundation of the program. Reading, language skills, mathematics.

Program designed to meet interests and needs of many different kinds of functionally illiterate groups.

Systems approach, involving a variety of independent, small-group, and instructor-guided activities; grade levels 0–12.

b. *Pre-GED: Basic Writing Skills*
Basic Social Studies
Basic Science
Basic Reading
Basic Math
Reading level: 5–7.

Each book covers all the subjects found in the actual GED test.

c. *Dr. Spello,* 2/e
Reading level: 4–5.

Groups words according to sound-symbol and structural relationships.

5. New Reader's Press, division of Laubach Literacy International, Box 131, Syracuse, NY 13210.

a. *News for You*

A weekly newspaper for adults with the latest information about current national and world events. Includes features on sports, health, legal matters, working and jobs, how to cope; in a form easier to read than local newspapers.

Edition A — Reading level: 4–5
Edition B — Reading level: 5–6

6. Science Research Associates (SRA), 155 North Wacker Dr., Chicago, IL 60606.

a. *New Computational Skills Development Kit*
Grades 6–adult.

A good supplement for any mathematics program. Helps students discover weaknesses and strengthen skills in addition, subtraction, multiplication, and division of whole numbers, fractions, decimals, and percents.

7. Scott Foresman and Company, Lifelong Learning Division, 1900 E. Lake Ave., Glenview, IL 60025.

a. *Adult Reading: Comprehension*

Twenty-four titles on four themes (people, coping, cultures, messages), with six sixty-four–page paperback books per theme ranging from second- to sixth-grade–equivalent reading levels. Instructor's guide.

b. *Adult Readers Library*

Fourteen short, pleasure-reading books especially for adults, which are high-interest and low reading level (3.5–5.0).

c. *Essential Mathematics for Life*

Four titles (whole numbers; decimals and fractions; percents, graphs, and measurement; basic arithmetic review, geometry, algebra), which feature low reading level, life-skills applications, and self-testing approach. Sample duplicating master kit and instructor's guide.

d. *English That Works*
Prevocational English as a Second Language program that emphasizes getting and keeping a job.

References

Dennis, L. J., and Eaton, W. E. (Eds.). *George S. Counts: Educator for a New Age.* Carbondale: Southern Illinois Press, 1980.

Freire, P. *Pedagogy of the Oppressed.* New York: Seabury, 1970.

Greenleigh Associates, Inc. *Field Test and Evaluation of Selected Adult Basic Education Systems.* New York: Greenleigh Associates, Inc., 1966.

Hechinger, F. M. "About Education: Psychologist Sees a Key to Learning in Managing 'Unsolvable' Problems." *The New York Times,* August 18, 1981, p. C5.

Knowles, M. *Basic Skills Catalog.* Chicago: Follett, 1982.

National Association for Public Continuing and Adult Education (NAPCAE). *Techniques for Teachers of Adults.* 1982, *23* (3); and 1980, *20* (5).

Florence W. Carmen graduated from Syracuse University. She taught in the Job Corps, was a consultant in adult basic education at Oswego State College, and was a speaker at a workshop for tutors of migrant workers. In 1965 she was selected as a teacher for the Greenleigh Associates Field Test and Evaluation of Selected Adult Basic Education Systems. Since then she has been teaching adult basic education and high school equivalency in Syracuse, New York.

In the evaluation of materials, the type of medium is much less important than the characteristics of the medium and of the learners who use it.

Evaluating Educational Materials

Richard L. Holloway

Evaluation in continuing education has become an increasingly vital issue and will be even more so in the face of economic stress and social pressures. Program evaluation has been the major emphasis, and much has been written on this subject in adult and continuing education (Grotelueschen, 1980). There are many reasons for program evaluation and a large number of variables to consider in designing evaluations of continuing education programs. Program elements and program perspectives, as discussed by Grotelueschen (1980), help the program evaluator design evaluations suited to various purposes.

One frequently overlooked or underemphasized element in a program is the material used and the effect it has on program outcomes. This chapter concerns the evaluation of educational materials. Rather than focusing on specific types of materials such as books, films, or other media, the emphasis will be on the application of a body of knowledge that considers characteristics of materials and their evaluation in light of learner attributes. The method by which to do this is referred to as aptitude by treatment interaction (ATI) because it considers effects of treatment on learners. In the context of this chapter, materials are seen as the treatment that interacts with certain learner attributes.

Media Research

For years, researchers have attempted to investigate the relative effectiveness of media and combinations of media and have made various other

The author thanks Carol A. Carrier for helpful insights and suggestions.

J. P. Wilson (Ed.). *Materials for Teaching Adults: Selection, Development, and Use.* New Directions for Continuing Education, no. 17. San Francisco: Jossey-Bass, March 1983.

mixed-media comparisons. Clark (1982) recently pointed out in a book review of sixty years of media research that such attempts have proved fruitless because they have missed the point of instructional effectiveness. Researching the effectiveness of media by comparing one medium to another to try to determine which is better ignores more fundamental questions about the attributes of those media.

A more fruitful, if more difficult, strategy is to thoroughly examine media attributes rather than the kind of medium (Snow, 1977; Tobias, 1982; Carter and Carrier, 1976). In other words, instead of pitting medium against medium, the researcher can examine instructional variables such as pacing, sequencing, time on task, or level of organization as a way of examining the effective components of a medium. Such strategies are more useful to evaluators of instructional media because the evaluator is able to consider the unique characteristics of the medium and its effectiveness for a particular audience. In other words, the ideal situation is to have an evaluator match instructional types to learner types. As in many areas of investigation, this ideal has not become reality; however, significant steps have been taken toward achieving what Clark (1975) has referred to as a "taxonomy of media attributes" that uses ATI research methods.

ATI seeks to provide information regarding the effectiveness of medium characteristics for a particular kind of learner. To accomplish this goal, methods are used that compare these characteristics to one another by correlating outcomes with a defined learner attribute and finding out if differences exist between several media characteristics. Figure 1 illustrates how this principle is handled methodologically. The figure shows that for material A, there is a strong relationship between aptitude x and outcome y; this relationship is in a positive direction. For material B, which may be different from A only in that it lacks the media attribute in question, a very different relationship is present between aptitude x and outcome y. It appears as though there may be an opposite relationship than the one present for A. If differences in treatment characteristics have been carefully controlled and learner characteristics precisely measured, we may conclude that the change in relationship is due to the interaction between the learner characteristic and the attribute manipulated in the instructional materials. Knowledge of these interactions may be extremely useful in evaluating the relative merits of either of the materials for learners with these characteristics. Moreover, this information can help the instructor to learn more about learner requirements and desirable attributes in instructional materials.

Application

To better explain these concepts, let us examine a specific study of the relationship between a learner characteristic (reading ability) and outcome (comprehension of information) given two reading difficulty levels of instruction (Eaton and Holloway, 1980).

Figure 1. Comparison of Medium Characteristics by
Correlating Outcomes with Defined Learner Attributes

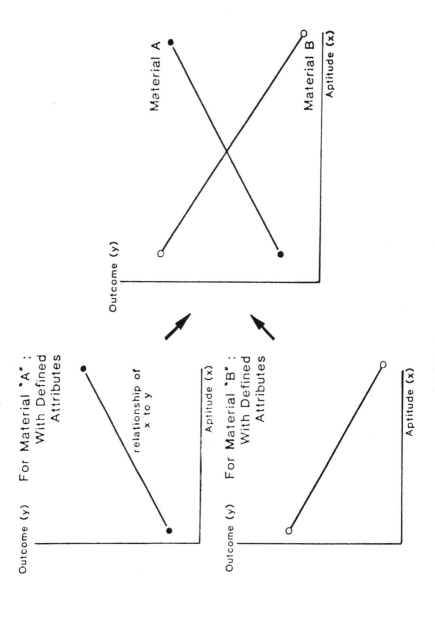

An important aspect of adult medical patient care is the information provided to adult patients about the drugs they use. A relatively simple but overlooked component of such materials is their readability. Many recent studies have shown that existing patient information provided by drug companies is often not understood by patients either because it is too technical or, perhaps, because patients are incapable of comprehending the information provided (Liguori, 1978).

To test the usefulness of a particular kind of patient information (drug package inserts), an ATI study was constructed that compared the readability of patient information at two difficulty levels (fifth-grade reading level and tenth-grade reading level). All other aspects of these materials were identical, including the content of the materials. In addition, the reading ability of subjects (the pertinent learner characteristics) was tested using the ABLE test of reading ability (Karlson and others, 1967). The purpose of the study was to find out if the materials of lower readability were able to influence comprehension of the materials for subjects of differing reading ability. It was also useful to know whether either of these types of materials was appropriae for all patients or if some learners would benefit only from one or the other. For instance, high-ability learners might be insulted by the fifth-grade materials and this might reduce comprehension.

The findings from this study suggested that two principles were operating. First, regardless of the level of readability of the materials, outcomes on a test of comprehension were highly dependent on reading ability. Both materials showed correlations with outcomes. Second, regardless of an individual's reading ability, the comprehension scores were higher for the fifth-grade–level materials than for the tenth-grade–level materials.

As a result of the study, the investigators were able to make several important conclusions: (1) Drug information should be written in the simplest possible manner, regardless of reading ability; (2) materials written at a higher level of readability are more dependent on reading ability, favoring high-ability learners; and (3) individual differences (in this case, reading ability) must be considered in the design of instructional materials because there are strong relationships between ability and outcome, regardless of the materials. Even though the interaction was not significant in this study, it is clear that the information about learner characteristics and media attributes was very useful. In addition to the comprehension test, subjects were asked about the clarity of the materials. Here, a strong interaction between reading ability and the readability of the materials was present, which indicated that the perception of clarity is even more influenced by the different materials than the outcome test. This finding also underscores the importance of using more than one outcome measure to assess the effectiveness of various materials for different learners.

Equally evident from this sample is the limitation of dealing with a single instructional characteristic and limited learner characteristics. If possible, the evaluator of educational materials should attend to a broader range of instructional variables and learner characteristics. These variables and characteristics should be chosen on the basis of expected relationships. The next sections will describe some considerations for choosing expected meaningful learner characteristics and instructional variables.

Using Research to Guide Evaluation Methods

The guidelines that follow will help to apply ATI research principles to evaluation. These planning phases will help the evaluator draw sound conclusions about the effectiveness of educational materials.

1. *Identify the nature and scope of the content area.* A clear description of the content being taught and its scope is an important starting place in the ATI evaluation. This content identification will help locate pertinent literature and help define the dimensions of the treatment.

Well-defined objectives must be obtained to guide the selection of relevant outcome measures as well as to define the nature of the treatment. Objectives must be stated to help draw conclusions about the materials under consideration and other similar materials. The ability to generalize from the conclusions is enhanced by being as specific as possible.

2. *Identify the structural elements of the materials.* Obvious structural characteristics of the materials, such as the use of self-pacing, requirements for student-initiated projects or conferences with teachers, or the quantity of interaction with technology, may signal a need to look at the interactive effects of particular aptitudes or personality dimensions. For example, are the materials designed to facilitate the progress of the independent, self-directed individual more than one with less self-determination? A program with this structural difference may signal a need to examine the locus of control (Rotter, 1966) or some other personality variable related to self-reinforcement.

3. *Identify learner characteristics.* Participants may differ in the degree of program-relevant knowledge and skills that they process upon entry. Paper-and-pencil as well as performance-based pretesting will provide indices of this important variable. Tobias (1976) has found that the level of preknowledge is related to success under instructional treatments that vary with respect to the degree of instructional support provided for the learner. It appears that students with great preknowledge have less need for instructional support devices of various kinds (such as constructed responses or feedback) than those with lower levels of preknowledge. Finding these differences in pre-entry states may explain differential performance on outcome measures.

4. *Identify personality characteristics.* As was alluded to earlier, various personality characteristics may have impact on the instructional approach. For example, locus of control has been found to be an important variable in the comparison of teacher-controlled and self-paced instruction. Students who differ on locus-of-control scores tend to differ, both affectively and cognitively, in their responses to the treatment.

What Are the Critical Outcome Measures to Be Collected?

Too often, outcome measures are chosen because of convenience. Cognitive measures are useful and probably necessary in the evaluation of educational materials, but other meaures—and not just affective ones—should be used to ensure that outcomes are related to aptitude measures and the unique characteristics of the materials. Four categories of outcomes can be effectively related to aptitudes and instructional methods: cognitive (What new knowledge has the learner acquired?), performance (What new skills and/or behaviors have been learned?), attitudinal (In what ways has the learner changed his or her attitude?), and process (What appear to be the interactions, dynamics, and effects of materials in a broader sense?).

Relating these categories of outcomes to instructional components (content and structure) and learner characteristics (preknowledge, personality, predisposition) allows the evaluator to attribute change more accurately to particular kinds of ATI. This is critical while attempting to compensate for the relative lack of experimental controls that can be used in the evaluation of instructional materials in most continuing education settings.

This process can be conducted for each of the four kinds of outcomes desired (performance, attitude, cognitive, process) and will then allow the evaluator to describe the attributes of the materials and their effects more explicitly.

Conclusions

The ATI approach to evaluation can be very beneficial. Instead of merely describing the outcomes achieved from instructional materials, many attributes can be assessed and related to outcomes. This understanding of relationships can serve both to describe the structural elements of materials and to predict the kinds of participants who may be successful using materials of differing instructional characteristics. The results of such a process as ATI evaluation expand questions for the evaluator beyond the realm of "Which materials are better?" A more precise question for the evaluator now might be "Which components of these materials are better for which kinds of students, and what outcomes are produced?"

References

Carter, J., and Carrier, C. "Prose Organization and Recall." *Contemporary Educational Psychology*, 1976, *1*, 329-345.

Clark, R. E. "Consulting a Taxonomy of Media Attributes for Research Purposes." *AV Communications Review*, 1975, *23*, 197-215.

Clark, R. E. "Review of Media Instruction: Sixty Years of Research." *Educational Communications and Technology Journal*, 1982, *30*, 60.

Eaton, M. L., and Holloway, R. L. "Patient Comprehension of Written Drug Information." *American Journal of Hospital Pharmacy*, 1980, *37*, 240-243.

Grotelueschen, A. D. "Program Evaluation." In A. B. Knox and Associates, *Developing, Administering, and Evaluating Adult Education.* San Francisco: Jossey-Bass, 1980.

Karlson, B., Gardner, E. F., and Madden, R. *Adult Basic Learning Examination.* New York: Harcourt Brace Jovanovich, 1967.

Liguori, S. "A Quantitative Assessment of the Readability of PPI's." *Drug Intelligence in Clinical Pharmacy,* 1978, *12,* 712-716.

Rotter, J. B. "Generalized Expectancies for Internal Versus External Control of Reinforcement." *Psychological Monographs,* 1966, *80* (1), Whole No. 609.

Snow, R. E. "Individual Differences and Instructional Theory." *Educational Researcher,* 1977, *6,* 11-15.

Tobias, S. "Achievement Treatment Interactions." *Review of Educational Research,* 1976, *46,* 61-74.

Tobias, S. "When Do Instructional Methods Make a Difference?" *Educational Researcher,* 1982, pp. 4-9.

Richard L. Holloway is associate professor of education in the Department of Family Practice and Community Health at the University of Minnesota. He serves as the department's director of curriculum development and coordinates research activities for the Faculty Report Program and residents.

How do I know when to use what, with whom, and why?

Where Do We Grow from Here: Synthesis and Discussion

John P. Wilson

Helping people learn is the primary objective of teaching. How to know when to do what, with whom, and why sets the parameters for organizing instruction effectively to achieve this aim.

One major purpose of this sourcebook is to provide examples of various educational materials and to describe their use in rather specific contexts. Another purpose is to provide some background information about materials, either in the form of research findings regarding their development and effective use, or in the form of personal, subjective observation and experience. A third purpose is to broaden perspectives on what constitutes educational materials.

Some of the preceding chapters are mostly concerned with using existing materials (Goldman, Chapter Nine), while others focus more on developing materials (Geib and McMeen, Chapter Two; Miller, Chapter Three; Thomas, Chapter Six; Heaney, Chapter Five; Rydell, Chapter Eight; Wedemeyer, Chapter Seven; Holloway, Chapter Twelve). Additionally, adapting materials (Charles, Chapter Ten) and combining various resources with materials (Simonson, Chapter Four) are discussed. Finally, various factors within the overall educational enterprise, such as learner characteristics, and the nature of educational material, subject matter, goals, and resources are presented (Meierhenry, Chapter One).

J. P. Wilson (Ed.). *Materials for Teaching Adults: Selection, Development, and Use.* New Directions for Continuing Education, no. 17. San Francisco: Jossey-Bass, March 1983.

All of the information presented in these chapters has implications for the development, adaptation, selection, and use of educational materials in continuing education settings. Many implications have been discussed in the respective chapters.

The intent of this concluding chapter is to synthesize information presented in the preceding chapters. The goal is to organize the information; to put it into some kind of framework so that it may be useful to selecting, adapting, or developing materials across varying continuing education settings.

The discussion is in three parts: What constitutes educational material, elements in the educational enterprise that affect or are affected by material, and how to select materials.

Instructional Materials

There are many different kinds of and uses for instructional materials. The most common materials include textbooks, worksheets, observation guides, films, photographs, short readings as handouts, film strips, and video and audio tapes. Ordinarily, materials are seen to serve several purposes: as a supplement to instruction (worksheets), as givers of information (textbooks), and as the entire instructional system (for example, a correspondence course).

Most of these kinds of materials were discussed in the preceding chapters. The three purposes of materials noted above were also assumed. A more general perception of educational material also surfaced. Educational material can be thought of as anything that, in itself, provides information or, by association, generates information. For example, for Heaney (Chapter Five), educational material is whatever a community decides is important to lift itself from its own state of oppression. Such material might demonstrate the extent to which the people limit themselves in their views of their social, psychological, and physical environment; their attitudes about their lives in general; and, most importantly, their perceptions of what they can and will do to improve their situation. For Thomas (Chapter Six), computers can coordinate the work environment closely enough in nature and time to facilitate personal integration by learners. Finally, Carmen (Chapter Eleven) refers to literature that her ABE participants produced about themselves and their life experiences. This material helps these learners in their literacy skills. It provides them a basis for self-expression and reflection that can lead to increased desire and ability to learn. Thus, the major purpose of material is to help learners internalize whatever needs to be learned, for without this, whether learning has occurred at all remains in question.

This broadened perspective of educational materials and their purpose greatly expands the pool from which to select materials for any given purpose. This expansion increases the need for giving special consideration to certain elements within the educational enterprise, and additionally, to attend to the effects of this interrelationship between these elements on the effectiveness of materials while selecting, developing, or using them.

Elements in the Educational Enterprise

Each preceding chapter addresses at least one element in the educational enterprise that affects or is affected by materials. Some relationships of these elements to materials development, selection, adaptation, and use are discussed. A synthesis of these discussions suggests a set of features common to all continuing education settings. These features can be called method, learner, and content goals. Although discussed individually in earlier chapters, these features are actually intricately interdependent. Thus, it seems useful to not only focus on them individually, but also to examine their interdependencies in selecting, developing, or using educational materials.

There have been many attempts to clarify parameters and foundations of adult and continuing education. One such attempt presents a three-dimensional model that depicts three elements of an educational enterprise and their transactional relationships (Boyd and Apps, 1980). The model is visually presented in Figure 1. These three elements correspond synonymously to method, learner, and content goals. Thus the model helps to organize information in this sourcebook and to generalize about applications of it with materials development, selection, and use across various continuing education settings.

Method. Meierhenry (Chapter One) concludes that the choice of materials is affected by the way in which the educational setting is organized. This means that method has some relationship to materials use. The term *method* is meant to include the organizational attributes of the educational enterprise.

Three methods are discussed in the chapters of this book. Wedemeyer (Chapter Seven) and Rydell (Chapter Eight) discuss materials used in individualized settings (correspondence study, self-directed study). Meierhenry (Chapter One), Geib and McMeen (Chapter Two), and Carmen (Chapter Eleven) discuss materials useful for teaching in groups. Heaney (Chapter Five) presents procedures for developing and using videotaped material within a community setting. These examples correspond to the three modes in Figure 1: individual, group, and community.

It is tempting at this point to make some generalizations about the implications of method for materials use and development. Some (Heaney, Chapter Five; Thomas, Chapter Six; Geib and McMeen Chapter Two) have done this. However, method by itself may be a relatively minor factor, but when coupled with the focus of the educational enterprise and goals, it increases in importance.

Learner. A second dimension of the model in Figure 1 is called *client focus.* Client focus identifies whether the benefactor of the education is to be an individual, a group, or the community.

Wedemeyer (Chapter Seven) underscores the importance of recognizing the individuality of learners and the propensity for idiosyncratic learning. The implication is that materials need to be directed more toward individuals than the masses, and that it thus requires a great deal of knowledge about an

Figure 1: Three Interdependent Elements in Adult and Continuing Education Programs*

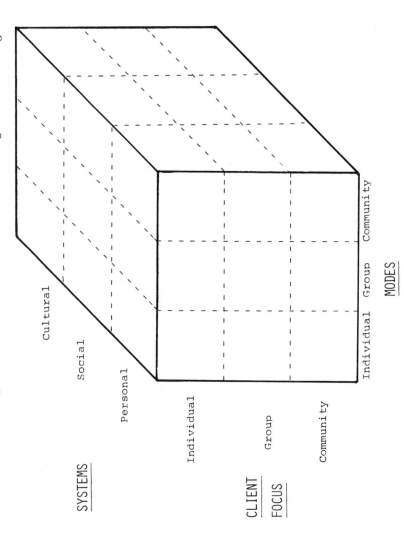

Source: Based on material presented in Boyd and Apps (1980).

individual's history, motivations, situation, goals, and so on to be effective in teaching. Thomas (Chapter Six) implies that computer models of instruction can be focused on the individual's life history as well. Rydell (Chapter Eight) emphasizes materials for use by individuals in self-directing their learning.

Some authors (Geib and McMeen, Chapter Two; Miller, Chapter Three; Simonson, Chapter Four; Charles, Chapter Ten; Carmen, Chapter Eleven; and Holloway, Chapter Twelve) base their discussions on materials for use in group settings. Their assumptions seem to be that such groups are comprised of individuals, therefore materials should be directed toward individuals. Whereas the main benefactor of most group instructional settings is, in fact, the individual, there are occasions when individuals enter group settings (classes, lectures) to learn for the main purpose of benefiting a group or community of which the individual is a member. Further, there may be occasions when the focus of instruction is on the group of participants *as a group,* regardless of the individuality of the group members. An example would be when a collection of individuals come to a group setting to learn how they can work more effectively together.

Finally, Heaney (Chapter Five) presents a case where the main beneficiary of the educational experience is an entire community. Granted, individuals were involved and did the learning, but their main purpose was improving the life of their community. Clearly if one is interested in teaching a group how to be a more effective group, different techniques of instruction and accompanying materials would be more useful than those implemented while teaching individuals such things as money management or engine repair. Similarly, different procedures and materials would be required if the focus were on a community as main beneficiary. However, a third factor comes into play along with the method and main beneficiary. This factor relates to goals.

Content Goals. The third dimension in the model in Figure 1 is called *system.* There are three systems: personal, social, and cultural. It is posited that one of these systems plays a more prominent role than the others in participant orientations. Certain chapters in this sourcebook exemplify these systems and illustrate how the dominant system may be translated into goals.

Goldman (Chapter Nine) focused on self-assessment materials and procedures. Therein, he discusses occasions when self-assessment instruments are relevant and what they may accomplish. Accomplishments may include changing careers, starting a business, or changing one's personal life in some way. This clearly exemplifies the personal system as a motivator of some continuing education participants, and has many implications for what kinds of materials may be useful.

The social system as central to the educational enterprise is exemplified by the kinds of projects discussed by Heaney (Chapter Five). Clearly, the Rockford Project was designed and implemented in special ways to enhance the status of a specific community. The project focused on establishing a community and developing the capacity of community members to communicate and cooperate among themselves and with local groups and the at-large city government.

None of the other chapters in this sourcebook seem to be directly attuned to the social system as central to participant orientation. However, individuals may be learning at a distance, enrolled in certain group programs, or taking on self-directed learning projects as a way to learn how they can contribute to the betterment of a given social system of which they are a part. Further, none of the chapters appears to point toward materials use in settings where the central orientation of participants is cultural. An exception could be Heaney's work (Chapter Five). But, as in the case of the social system, it is possible that individuals and even small groups of people are participating in various continuing education programs for mainly cultural development within one or several social settings.

Selecting Materials

Many implications for materials selection, development, adaptation, and use are suggested throughout this sourcebook. A synthesis of these suggestions adds further insights. There is no prescription for selecting, adapting, and using materials in all settings. This can only be done after first identifying a specific setting with a specific set of learners. But how is this to be accomplished?

Carmen's (Chapter Eleven) and Wedemeyer's (Chapter Seven) suggestion of dialogue with learners is an important tool. Some of the self-assessment devices and instruments discussed by Goldman (Chapter Nine) can be considered as other tools, and perhaps Thomas's (Chapter Six) views regarding the use of computers and their capabilities for personalizing learning would be helpful. Finally, Heaney (Chapter Five) suggests that learners create their own educational materials. This may be the most effective procedure in many cases.

The decisions might be further enhanced, however, by reflecting on whether the materials are to be supplemental to a program, information-giving, or representative of the entire instructional system. Viewing materials as aids to the internalization of content opens the door to a greater variety of material and more uses for it, regardless of the setting.

Perhaps most important, decisions about materials need to take into account the intricate relationships between method, primary beneficiary, and the orientation system of central concern to the learner. For example, suppose the community is seen as the main beneficiary of a given continuing education program. Additionally, the method of instruction is the community type and the central orientation relates to the social system. Materials development and use in this case would most appropriately be of the sort discussed by Heaney (Chapter Five). On the other hand, suppose a specific group of people, for whatever reason, need to work together as a team, and hence enroll, as a unit, in a continuing education program on team development. The central orientation of the group would most likely be the social system; that is, how they can operate collectively. The main beneficiary would be the group, rather than the individuals who comprise the group. Materials for teaching in this circumstance would be most effective if they focus on helping the group to become a team rather than helping them to know what makes a team and how teams behave. Materials of this sort are abundant in publications such as Structured Experiences for Human Relations Training (Pfieffer and Jones, 1969–1981).

Finally, suppose a number of people enroll in a program for some personal, individualized reason such as developing individual strengths in interpersonal communication. Whereas the method of instruction may be via a group, the chief beneficiary is the individual and the system orientation is personal. Here, the most effective materials would be the individually guided, self-assessment types and forms discussed by Wedemeyer (Chapter Seven), Rydell (Chapter Eight), and Goldman (Chapter Nine).

Conclusions

This chapter has specified certain critical elements within the educational enterprise that influence, or are influenced by, materials. They were identified on the bases of discussions in other chapters, and include a broadened perspective of what constitutes educational materials, methods, learner and content goals.

Earlier chapters discuss these elements in more specific, although isolated, ways, and with more specific reference points. The combinations of method, main beneficiary, and central orientation are many, and demonstrate the complexities involved in continuing education. Although each is important individually, their interdependencies are critical to selecting, adapting, and developing materials.

In total, this sourcebook provides a foundation on which continuing educators can establish a rationale and procedures for selecting, developing, or adapting a wide array of educational materials. There are apparently more materials available for certain combinations of various elements in educational settings than other combinations, and some are more adaptable to certain combinations. What may be needed now are more materials that focus on social and cultural orientation systems where groups and communities are to be the main beneficiaries.

References

Boyd, R. D., and Apps, J. W. *Redefining the Discipline of Adult Education.* San Francisco: Jossey-Bass, 1980.
Pfieffer, W., and Jones, J. *A Handbook of Structured Experiences for Human Relations Training.* (8 volumes.) San Diego: University Associates, 1969–1981.

John P. Wilson is professor of adult and extension education and extension specialist-education at Iowa State University. He graduated from the University of Wisconsin-Madison, where he studied instructional theory, group dynamics, and learning in adult education. He has developed and published many educational materials and workbooks. He has also used these materials extensively for teaching in various continuing education programs.

Index

A

Abstraction: and educational background, 7; for older learners, 81
Adult basic education (ABE): analysis of materials for, 85–93; bibliographies for, 90–93; choosing and evaluating materials for, 87–88; and creative writing, 89–90; life-centered education for, 88; teachers and materials for, 85–86
Allison, R. W., 33, 34
Alternate Media Center, 40
Amb, T., 14, 19
Apps, J. W., 105, 106n, 109
Aptitude by treatment interaction (ATI): analysis of, 95–101; application of, 96, 98–99; and evaluation methods, 99; and media research, 95–97; and outcome measures, 100
Arenberg, D., 81, 83
Attitudinal outcomes: analysis of media for, 29–35; and credibility, 31–32; and emotional arousal, 33–34; guidelines for, 30–34; and involvement, 32; and new information, 31; and postinstruction discussions, 32–33; realism, relevance, and stimulation for, 30–31
Audio-Assisted Independent Study, 15, 18
Audiotape and videotape materials: analysis of, 13–19; development procedures for, 16; examples of, 15–16; rationale for, 14–15; rhetorical elements of, 17; verbal material in, 16–17
August, B., 91
Aural surroundings, for older learners, 80
Ausubel, D. P., 17, 18

B

Barasovska, J., 90
Barndt, D., 44

Bell, B., 83
Berger, E. J., 14, 18
Bickel, R. F., 14, 18
Billings, T. E., 24, 27
Birren, J., 82, 83
Booth, G. D., 30, 34
Botwinick, J., 78, 79, 80, 81, 83, 84
Boyd, R. D., 105, 106n, 109
Brain Teaser, and problem solving, 49–52
Bray, R. M., 34
Breglio, V. J., 34
Breneman, D., 25, 27
Broadside TV, 40
Bruner, J., 85
Burke, K., 17, 18
Burke, W. W., 14, 18
Buros, O. K., 70, 74
Burrichter, A. W., 33, 34

C

California, reading study in, 85–86
Campbell, D. P., 70, 74
Campeau, P. L., 22, 27
Career Development Inventory, 72
Career Maturity Inventory, 72
Carey, R., 75
Cargill, O., 19
Carmen, F. W., 1, 85–93, 104, 105, 107, 108
Carr, V. H., Jr., 16, 18
Carrier, C. A., 95n, 96, 100
Carter, J., 96, 100
CETA, 42, 64
Challenge for Change, 39
Chamberlain, M., 6, 11
Charles, D. C., 1, 77–84, 103, 107
Chicago, education and change in, 40, 41
Clark, R. E., 96, 100
Cognitive styles, of adult learners, 8–9
Coldevin, G. O., 32, 34
College Board, 71
Color vision, by older learners, 79

111

Communications for Change, 40, 41
Community Video, 40
Computers: and adult basic education, 88–89; implications of trends in, 5–6; as learning environment, 48; and problem solving, 47–52; for self-assessment, 72
Coolican, P. M., 62, 67
Council for the Advancement of Experiential Learning (CAEL), 63
Counts, G. S., 87
Crites, J. O., 72, 74
Croft, R. G., 30, 34
Cross, K. P., 21, 27, 61, 62, 67

D

Dark adaptation, by older learners, 79
Datiles, U. P., 16, 18
Dennis, L. J., 87, 93
Denver Public Library, 64
Depth perception, by older learners, 79
Dewey, C. R., 71, 75
DISCOVER II, 63
Domyahn, R. A., 33, 34
Donaldson, J., 30, 34
Dossin, C., Jr., 26, 27
Drug package inserts, readability of, 98

E

Eaton, M. L., 96, 100
Eaton, W. E., 87, 93
Education: content goals in, 107–108; learner in, 105, 107; method in, 105
Edutek Corporation, 49
ENCORE, 63
Erickson, C. W. H., 32, 34
Evans, C., 44

F

Fadiman, C., 91
Fay, F. A., 33, 34
Feldman, R. M., 79, 83
Feshbach, S., 33, 35
Figler, H., 74, 75
Fisher, H. L., 24, 25, 27
Fogo Island Project, and social change, 39–40

Fozard, J. L., 79, 83
Freire, P., 6, 11, 23, 27, 39, 44, 86, 93

G

Gagné, R. M., 17, 19
Ganschow, L. H., 30, 35
Gardner, E. F., 101
Geib, P., 1, 2, 13–19, 103, 105, 107
Gellatt, H. B., 71, 75
Globe Book Co., 91
Goldman, B. A., 32, 35
Goldman, L., 2, 69–75, 103, 107, 108, 109
Golomb, S. W., 47–48, 52
Greenleigh Associates, 85, 86, 93
Gross, R., 54, 59
Grotelueschen, A. D., 95, 101
Gwyn, S., 40, 44

H

Hall, L. G., 71, 75
Hall Occupational Orientation Inventory, 71
Hanson, J. C., 70, 74
Harris-Bowlsbey, J. A., 63
Hawes, E., 31, 35
Heaney, T. W., 2, 6, 37–45, 103, 104, 105, 107, 108
Hearing, changes in, with aging, 79–80
Hechinger, F. M., 85, 93
Hemispheric specialization, in adult learners, 9–10
Herman, S., 44
Higher Education Act, Title I-A of, 42
Holland, J., 71, 75
Holloway, R. L., 2, 95–101, 103, 107
Holmberg, B., 54, 59
Holmes, N., 56–57, 59
Hopkins, J., 40, 44
Hopkinson, P., 39, 44
Howard, J., 91
Howe, L., 74, 75

I

Institute for Life Skills Employability Skills Series, 91
Interactive media, for liberatory education, 39–43

Interests, self-assessment of, 70–71
Irrelevancy, for older learners, 81

J

Jamestown Publishers, 91
Janis, I. L., 33, 35
Jones, A., 59
Jones, G. E., 35
Jones, J., 109
Jordaan, J. P., 75
Jouko, C., 31, 35

K

Karlson, B., 98, 101
Katz, M. R., 72, 75
Kirschenbaum, H., 74, 75
Kirk, J., 44
Kishler, J. P., 31, 35
Klapper, H. L., 14, 19, 30, 35
Klingensmith, J. E., 14, 19
Knowles, M. S., 62, 67, 86, 93
Knowlton, J., 31, 35
Kolb, D. E., 8, 11

L

Langford, M., 23, 25, 27
Lanz, M., 21, 23, 27
Learning: elements in, 21–22; schooling related to, 53–54; transfer of, 49, 65–66
Learning styles: of adult learners, 8; and self-directed learning, 65
Levonian, E., 30, 31, 35
Liberatory education, interactive media for, 39–43
Libraries, and self-directed learning, 64, 66
Light sensitivity, in older learners, 79
Liguori, S., 98, 101
Lindeman, R. H., 75
Linguistics, and materials development, 57–58
Lippitt, G. L., 14, 19
Literacy, materials for, 85–93
Literacy Volunteers of America, 91
London, education and change in, 40
Loomis, J., 19

M

McCarthy, B. F., 8, 11
McFarland, R. A., 79, 83
McFarlane, A. M., 30, 35
McGraw-Hill Book Co., 91–92
McMeen, G. R., 1, 2, 13–19, 103, 105, 107
Madden, R., 101
Marino, D., 44
Marylhurst College for Lifelong Learning, and self-directed learning, 64
Materials: for adult basic education, 85–93; aptitude by treatment interaction evaluation of, 95–101; and attitudinal outcomes, 29–35; audiotaped and videotaped, 13–19; content of, 10; development of, for self-directed learners, 61–67; guidelines for developing, 56–58; issues in developing, 58–59; for nontraditional study, 53–60; for older learners, 77–84; for problem solving, 47–52; purpose and goals of, 56, 65; rationale for variety in, 6; readability of, 56–57; selection of, 103–109; selection variables for, 7–9; for self-assessment, 69–75; slide sets as, 21–27; and social change, 37–45; specialist role in developing, 54–56; synthesizing discussion of, 103–110; types of, 104; variety in, 5–11
Meierhenry, W. C., 1, 2, 5–11, 103, 105
Menne, J. W., 14, 19
Mental health, professional development materials in, 13–19
Metro Media, 40
Metropolitan State University, and self-directed learning, 64, 66
Meyers, M., 66, 67
Miller, D. J., 1, 21–27, 103, 107
Miller, H. R., 30, 34
Miller, W. C., 33, 35
Minneapolis Public Library, 66
Moldstad, J. A., 22, 27
Montreal, education and change in, 40
Moorhead State University: audiotape use at, 15; and self-directed learning, 64
Motivation, of older learners, 82–83
Murphy, P., 59
Myers, R. A., 75

N

National Association for Public Continuing and Adult Education (NAPCAE), 88, 93
National Endowment for the Humanities (NEH), 66
National Film Board of Canada, 39
National Research Council, 53, 59
New Jersey, reading study in, 86
New Reader's Press, 92
New York: education and change in, 40; library projects in, 64; reading study in, 86; writing in, 89
New York State Regents Competency Test, 89
New Zealand, readability study in, 56-57
Niemi, J., 43, 44
Non-Sexist Vocational Card Sort, 71
Nord, N. D., 14, 19
Northern Illinois University, and interactive media, 41

O

Oates, J., 55, 59
O'Brien, S. J., 32, 35
Office of Economic Opportunity, 85
Ohio University, and self-directed learning, 64
Ohliger, J., 39, 44
Okun, M. A., 82, 84
Older learners: analysis of changes in, 77-84; information processing by, 80-81; information receiving by, 78-80; noncognitive factors for, 82-83; responding by, 81-82; simplicity or complexity for, 8-81
Open University, course team concept at, 55
O'Shea, T., 59

P

Pacing, for older learners, 81
Paracelsus, P. A., 85n
Parallel Institute, 40
Peck, E. G., 24, 27
Penland, P., 62, 67
Peterson, R. C., 31, 35
Pfieffer, W., 109
PLATO, 64

Podolsky, S., 83
Pollack, T. C., 14, 19
Polya, G., 49, 51, 52
Popham, W. J., 14, 19
Presbycusis, in older learners, 79
Presbyopia, and older learners, 78-79
Problem solving: activities for skill development in, 49-52; background on, 47-49
Professional development: materials for, 13-19; program model for, 13-14

R

Rabbitt, P., 81, 84
Raedeke, A., 66, 67
Readability: for adult learners, 56-57; of drug package inserts, 98
Redundancy, and older learners, 81
Rees, J. N., 80, 84
Reger, S. N., 79, 83
Reich, P., 14, 19
Rockford Interactive Media Project, and social change, 40-43; 107-108
Rogers, R. W., 33, 35
Ross, W. L., 34
Rotter, J. B., 99, 101
Rubik's Cube, and problem solving, 47-48, 52
Rubinstein, M. F., 51, 52
Rydell, S. T., 2, 61-67, 103, 105, 107, 109

S

Sagamore Institute, 72
Scanlon, E., 54, 59
Schaie, K. W., 7, 11
Schooling, learning related to, 53-54
Science Research Associates (SRA), 92
Scott Foresman and Company, 92-93
Seiler, W., 30, 31-32, 35
Self-assessment: for adults, 69-75; background on, 69-70; for career planning and changing, 70-72; and follow-through, 74; for personal explorations, 72-74; workbooks for, 71
Self-directed learning: analysis of, 61-67; assumptions about, 65; characteristics of, 62-63; implications for, 66-67; material development for, 64-66; materials for teaching, 63-64; research on, 61-62

Self-Directed Search (SDS), 71
Simon, S., 74, 75
Simonson, M. R., 1, 29–35, 103, 107
Slide sets: analysis of, 21–27; audio for, 25–26; and learning, 21–22; planning for, 23–24; principles for, 22–27; production of, 24–26; use of, 26
Smith, P., 61–62, 67
Snow, R. E., 96, 101
Southeast Mental Health Center, professional development materials at, 13–19
Speech perception, by older learners, 80
Sperry, R. W., 9–10, 11
Stanford, G., 74, 75
Stanley, J., 14, 19
Stephans, S., 43, 44
Stereopsis, in older learners, 79
Stillwell, W. E., III, 35
Stimpson, D. V., 34
Strong-Campbell Interest Inventory (SCII), 70–71
Students: age of, 7; cognitive styles of, 8–9; educational background of, 7–8, 65; as educational element, 105–107; and hemispheric specialization, 9–10; and learning styles, 8, 65; older, changes in, 77–84; sex of, 9; teachers in relation to, 86–87
Super, D. E., 75
System of Interactive Guidance and Information (SIGI), 63, 72

T

Tarrier, R. B., 71, 75
Taylor, W. L., 56, 59
Teachers, students in relation to, 86–87
Technological model: afterthoughts on, 43–44; background on, 37–38; problems and alternatives for, 38–39
Tennessee, education and change in, 40
Texas at Austin, University of, functional literacy study at, 88
Theodore, T., 39, 45
Thomas, R. A., 2, 6, 47–52, 103, 104, 105, 107, 108
Thompson, A. S., 72, 75

Thorman, J. H., 14, 15, 19
Thorndike, E. L., 56
Thurstone, L. L., 29, 31, 35
Tobias, S., 96, 99, 101
Tough, A., 54, 59, 61, 62, 67
Trohanis, P. L., 22, 27
Tulsa City-County Library, 64

U

Union for Experimenting Colleges and Universities, and self-directed learning, 64
U.S. Office of Education, 85, 88

V

Values, self-assessment of, 73
Vancouver, education and change in, 40
Varenhorst, B., 75
Video technology, and social change, 37–45
Videotape. See Audiotape and videotape materials
Vincent, T., 59
Vision, changes in, with aging, 78–79
Vocational Card Sort (VCS), 71

W

Wagner, R. M. K., 43–44, 45
Wasson, J. B., 14, 15, 19
Wedemeyer, C. A., 1–2, 53–60, 103, 105, 108, 109
Weinstein, C., 91
Welfare Administration, 85
Whitelegg, L., 59
Wiegand, V. K., 17, 19
Williams, M. V., 83
Wilson, J. P., 1–3, 103–110
Wisconsin-Madison, University of, and interactive media, 41
Witkin, H. A., 8, 11
Wolf, E., 83
Woods, A. M., 83

Z

Zarbaugh, H., 19

From the Editor's Notes

An ever increasing amount of materials—printed, audio, visual, computer, and combinations of all of these—are currently available and being used in teaching adults. Some of these materials are more educationally sound than others, some need modification for use, and some are directly appropriate for adults. Given this increased availability of materials, adult and continuing educators are faced with the tasks of selecting the most effective materials, improvising where needed, and exploring various settings where some materials may be more effective than others. This volume of New Directions in Continuing Education *provides assistance to continuing educators in selecting among the wide array of educational materials available and provides information relevant to selecting, developing, adapting, evaluating, and using materials effectively.*

JOSSEY-BASS